Saints
Behaving
Badly

DOUBLEDAY

New York London Toronto Sydney Auckland

Saints
Behaving
Badly

The Cutthroats,

Crooks, Trollops,

Con Men, and Devil-Worshippers

Who Became Saints

Thomas J. Craughwell

Published in the United States by Image,
an imprint of the Crown Publishing Group,
a division of Penguin Random House LLC, New York.

www.crownpublishing.com

IMAGE is a registered trademark, and the "I" colophon
is a trademark of Penguin Random House LLC.

Originally published in hardcover in the United States by Doubleday,
a division of Penguin Random House LLC, New York in 2006.

Library of Congress Cataloging-in-Publication Data
is available on request.

ISBN 978-0-3853-6527-7

PRINTED IN THE UNITED STATES OF AMERICA

Book design by Nicola Ferguson

10   9   8   7   6   5   4   3   2   1

2016 Sterling Edition

For Alex and

Steven Mezzomo—

who never behave badly

Contents

Introduction

"Where is Mary Magdalene?"

I can see the reviewers' complaints now. How can you write a book about saints who started out as notorious sinners and omit the most famous converted sinner of all?

The short answer is "Mary Magdalene was not a notorious sinner."

Granted, centuries of paintings and sculptures have shown her draped in a loose red robe, her long, luxurious hair flowing free, her shoulders and sometimes even her breasts exposed—the very image of female sensuality. But art is not always evidence, especially so in this case. The inescapable fact remains that nowhere in the four gospels does it ever say that Mary Magdalene was a prostitute or in any other way sexually promiscuous. True, the gospels of Mark, Matthew, and Luke say that Christ cast seven devils out of Mary Magdalene, but that is no reason to assume that the demons made her "a sure thing." Christ cast devils out of plenty of men, too, but no one suggests that they were licentious. Luke does mention an anonymous "woman who was a sinner," but he never suggests this woman was Mary Magdalene.

Where, then, did we get this notion of Mary Magdalene as a harlot? There is evidence that in the first century of the Christian era Mary's hometown, Magdala, or el Mejdel, on the northwest shore of the Sea of Galilee, had an infamous reputation. About the year AD 75 the Roman authorities actually leveled the place and dispersed its depraved inhabitants. Perhaps the first Christians felt that anyone who came from el Mejdel had to be bad.

It is more likely, however, that Mary Magdalene the Prostitute is a composite of several New Testament women. There are lots of Marys in the gospels: Mary the mother of Jesus, Mary Magdalene, and Mary the sister of Martha and Lazarus being the most prominent. In an attempt to simplify things, at the end of the sixth century Pope St. Gregory the Great (c. 540–604) asserted that Luke's anonymous sinner, Mary the sister of Martha and Lazarus, and Mary Magdalene were all the same woman. The el Mejdel theory is plausible, but St.

Gregory is the most probable source for our misconceptions about the Magdalene.

In passing I'd like to mention that the current craze for rehabilitating/rediscovering/reimagining Mary Magdalene has done nothing to clarify the situation. About a year ago a group of Mary Magdalene aficionados managed to convince the pastor of a Catholic parish in northern New Jersey to let them use his church for a freewheeling service they wanted to conduct in honor of their favorite saint. The pastor gave them permission to use the building, but barred his parish clergy from presiding at, or even attending, the function. It was just as well. A local newspaper that covered the event reported that during the service a newly composed "Litany of Mary Magdalene" was read out to the attendees, listing Mary's supposed attributes. My personal favorite was the invocation "O, most inclusive one!"

Of course, suburban neo-Gnostics are not the only ones guilty of distorting the saints; perfectly orthodox Christians have been doing so for centuries. Christian art, whether in marble or in plaster, on canvas or on a laminated holy card, shows us saints who are blissful and pure, who appear incapable of ever uttering a cross word let alone spending years and years hip deep in mortal sin. In other words, most depictions of saints make sanctity look easy.

At least since the nineteenth century many authors have gone out of their way to sanitize the lives of the saints, often glossing over the more embarrassing cases with the phrase "he/she was once a great sinner." I don't doubt the hagiographers' good intentions, but I can't help thinking it is misguided to edit out the wayward years of a saint's life. In the early centuries of the Church and all through the Middle Ages writers of saints' lives were perfectly candid about saints whose early lives were far from saintly. It is from these ancient sources that we learn of the bloodbath St. Olga unleashed on her husband's assassins; of St. Mary of Egypt trolling the streets of Alexandria for new sexual conquests; of the obscenely rich St. Thomas Becket looking down at a poor man almost freezing to death in the street and refusing to give him his cloak.

The point of reading these stories is not to experience some tabloid thrill, but to understand how grace works in the world. Every day, all day long, God pours out his grace upon us, urging us, coaxing us, to turn away from everything that is base and cheap and unsatisfying, and turn toward the only thing that is eternal, perfect, and true—that is, himself.

What is a saint? A saint is a person who tries to imitate Jesus Christ, who strives to practice the virtues to a heroic degree. Lots of people are good, and some people around us show glimmers of saintliness from time to time, but a man or a woman whose entire life, all day, every day, is devoted to self-sacrificing good works and intense periods of conversation with God (commonly known as prayer), these individuals are rare indeed. Most of us will never know a saint.

Saints need not be infallibly perfect all the time. As I mentioned earlier, for the 2000 years of the Church's history, hagiographers gloried in the lives of great sinners who became great saints. Their message is reassuring: if these people can be saved, then so can you!

But just as the old storytellers did not whitewash the misdeeds of the saints, neither did they minimize the effort involved in conversion. A conversion experience is not magic; it is only the first step in a lifetime of striving to avoid the old sins, grow in virtue, and conform one's unruly, rebellious will to the will of God. All that is hard to do, as these stories will show.

Saints
Behaving
Badly

St. Matthew, Extortionist

[1st century]   *FEAST DAY: September 21*

No one likes taxes. But antitax animosity was especially intense in ancient Israel during the first century of the Christian era. In the gospels tax collectors (also known as publicans) are frequently mentioned in the same breath as harlots and sinners.

If tax collectors had a lousy reputation two thousand years ago, they deserved it. Under the Romans, the governor of each province was responsible for collecting the tax on land. Other taxes—on individuals, on personal property, on imports and exports—were subcontracted to private individuals who paid the Romans a fee in advance for the right to collect whatever Rome had levied on the conquered nations of its empire. These freelance tax collectors profited from this transaction by overcharging and extorting as much as they could get out of the taxpayers. The Romans didn't care—as long as they got the full balance of what was due. The Jews, on the other hand, cared quite a lot. In their eyes Jewish tax collectors were shameless crooks who committed the twofold crime of collaborating with heathens and preying upon their own people. Little wonder that the Jews of Christ's day regarded tax collectors with loathing.

Matthew, also called Levi in the gospels of St. Mark and St. Luke, was a tax collector at Capernaum, a Roman garrison town. He was sitting at his table in the customs house, shaking down his neighbors, when Jesus Christ walked by. Our Lord had just healed a paralyzed man; now he was about to reconcile a sinner. "Follow me," Christ said. To the surprise of the Roman guards, the clerks, and the taxpayers, Matthew got up, left the money where it lay on the table, turned his back on a life of government-sanctioned larceny, and joined the handful of men we know as the twelve apostles.

St. Luke's gospel tells us that Matthew celebrated his conversion by throwing an elaborate feast for Christ, the apostles, and a host of other guests. When the Pharisees complained that Jesus had no business dining with a notorious tax collector, Christ answered, "I came not to call the just, but sinners."

This is the only scene in the New Testament in which Matthew takes the spotlight.

From a very early date Christians attributed one of the gospels to St. Matthew. Although it comes first in the New Testament, in all probability St. Mark's is the oldest gospel, which almost certainly served as a source for Matthew. Matthew wrote for a Jewish audience; in his gospel he quotes frequently from the Hebrew scriptures to emphasize that Christ is the fulfillment of the prophecies. We owe to Matthew such unique features as St. Joseph's plan to divorce the Blessed Virgin Mary, the coming of the Magi to Bethlehem, King Herod's slaughter of the Holy Innocents, the Holy Family's flight into Egypt, a great part of the Sermon on the Mount, the parable of the sower, the metaphor of the sheep and the goats at the Last Judgment, the suicide of Judas, and the guards at Christ's tomb.

There is no reliable record of what Matthew did after the first Pentecost, when the apostles scattered to preach the gospel. He may have gone to Ethiopia, or to the region near the Caspian Sea—those two destinations appear most often in the old sources. There is even a dubious claim that St. Matthew went to Ireland. The truth is St. Matthew's later life is a mystery. Tradition says that he died a martyr, cut down with a sword as he said Mass. But we aren't even sure about that.

St. Dismas, Thief

[Died c. 30]   *FEAST DAY: March 25*

Christ was crucified between two thieves—all four gospels bear witness to this. But St. Luke's gospel fleshes out the scene a bit, giving "the Good Thief," the man tradition names Dismas, a few lines of dialogue.

The scene opens with the three men hanging on their crosses. "The Bad Thief," the man tradition names Gestas, reviles Jesus, saying, "If thou be the Christ, save thyself and us." That's when Dismas speaks up. "Neither dost thou fear God, seeing thou art under the same condemnation? And we indeed justly, for we receive the due reward of our deeds; but this man hath done no evil."

Then, addressing Christ, the dying Dismas says, "Lord, remember me when thou shalt come into thy kingdom."

Jesus replies, "Amen I say to thee, this day thou shalt be with me in paradise."

The scene is brief and poignant, and although the Good Thief doesn't say much, it is interesting to note that he has more lines than other, infinitely more popular New Testament saints. St. Jude, the enormously popular patron saint of impossible causes, is on record as speaking only once and very briefly in the gospels. Even stranger is the case of St. Joseph, Christ's foster father and the Blessed Virgin Mary's husband, who in the entire New Testament never says a single word.

From a very early date Christians found these silences and gaps in the stories of such significant players frustrating. An entire body of literature sprang up to answer the inevitable question "And then what happened?" The term for these narratives is apocrypha. They are writings that, in spite of their popularity with the early Christians, did not make it into the canon, the official list, of the books of the New Testament. Most of these works were omitted because they taught unorthodox doctrine (the so-called Gnostic gospels fall into this category). Other apocryphal works may have been perfectly orthodox in their understanding of the nature of Christ and his mission in the world but passed along stories about Mary's and Joseph's family backgrounds and the infancy and childhood of Christ that the early Church knew to be untrue or could not substantiate. The stories, or legends if you prefer, of St. Dismas are not theologically suspect, but it is certainly impossible at this point to say what, if anything, in these stories actually happened.

The earliest apocryphal work to attempt to flesh out the story of the Holy Family and St. Dismas is *The Arabic Gospel of the Infancy of the Savior*, dating from around 600. The book covers Mary and Joseph's journey into Egypt with the Christ Child to escape Judea's murderous King Herod, their return home to Nazareth a few years later, and Jesus' early childhood.

As Mary and Joseph wander through Egypt, looking for a safe place to call home, the local people warn them about a certain stretch of desert that is teeming with robbers. Hoping to pass without being detected, Mary and Joseph decide to travel by night. As they make their way through this dangerous territory, they see two highwaymen blocking the road ahead of them. Worse still, they realize that they have stumbled right into a robbers' camp: all around them dozens of cutthroats lie sleeping. The robbers watching the road are Dismas and Gestas.

Gestas is ready to get down to business and take anything of value the Holy Family has on them, but Dismas intervenes. "Let these persons go freely," Dismas says, "so that our comrades may not see them." It's a strange request from a hardened criminal, and Gestas dismisses it out of hand.

So Dismas makes his request more attractive. "Take to thyself these forty drachmas from me," Dismas says. Then he sweetens the deal by taking off his valuable belt and promising that to Gestas, too. The drachmas and the belt are an offer Gestas can't refuse, so he stands aside and lets the Holy Family go, free and unmolested.

Before they continue on their way, Mary prophesies to Dismas, "The Lord God will sustain thee by his right hand, and will grant thee remission of thy sins." But the Christ Child makes an even greater prophecy. "Thirty years hence, O my mother," he says, "these two robbers will be raised upon the cross along with me, Dismas on my right hand, and Gestas on my left: and after that day, Dismas shall go before me into paradise."

But this isn't the only ancient work to fill out the Dismas story. *The Gospel of Nicodemus*, a fourth-century apocryphal work, picks up Dismas's story where St. Luke's gospel leaves off. *The Gospel of Nicodemus* takes us down to the underworld during the three dark days Christ lay dead in his tomb.

According to Catholic theology, when Adam and Eve disobeyed God in Eden, the gates of Heaven were shut and would not be reopened until the Savior died and rose from the dead. During those long centuries the souls of the righteous went to Limbo, a level of Hell where they were spared the sufferings of the damned but were denied the beatific vision of God. When Christ descended into Hell, as the Apostles' Creed says, he liberated the souls of the just and led them to Heaven. In the Middle Ages this moment in the history of mankind's salvation was known as the Harrowing of Hell; it was a popular subject for mystery plays, with Christ entering like an all-powerful warlord ready to besiege a city. In spite of all the demons arrayed against him, Christ batters down the heavily fortified gates of Hell and releases the souls held captive there by the devil.

In *The Gospel of Nicodemus*, as the holy men and women who lived and died before the coming of Christ gather together for their long-awaited journey to Paradise, Enoch and Elijah see a man coming toward them dressed in vile clothes with the sign of the cross on his shoulders.

"Who art thou?" they ask, "for thine appearance is as of a robber; and wherefore is it that thou bearest a sign upon thy shoulders?"

The stranger is Dismas, of course, and he answers, "I was a robber, doing all manner of evil upon the earth. [But] I beheld the wonders in the creation which came to pass through the cross of Jesus when he was crucified, and I believed that he was the maker of all creatures and the almighty king, and I besought him, saying, 'Remember me, Lord, when thou comest into thy kingdom.' And forthwith he received my prayer, and said unto me, 'Verily I say unto thee, this day shalt thou be with me in paradise.' And he gave me the sign of the cross, saying: 'Bear this and go unto paradise.' "

At some point—when is hard to pinpoint—interest in St. Dismas segued into devotion. He became the patron saint of thieves specifically and criminals in general. The saint received a bit more attention in 1961 with the release of the movie *The Hoodlum Priest*, starring Don Murray as the tough-guy Jesuit Father Charles Dismas Clark, who served as a kind of missionary to street gangs and convicts. Under the patronage of St. Dismas, Catholic chaplains operate a ministry to incarcerated men and women.

As is often the case, we can see the depth of devotion to St. Dismas through the life of another saint. Father Emil Kapaun of Pilsen, Kansas, who is being promoted for sainthood, was a military chaplain during the Korean War. In November 1950 the North Koreans captured him and 1,200 American fighting men. The American POWs got so little food they were on the verge of starvation, so every night Father Kapaun crept out of the barracks to steal corn, millet, and soybeans from the guards' storehouse. Before Father Kapaun went out on his "foraging" forays, he prayed to St. Dismas, the Good Thief.

St. Callixtus, Embezzler

[Died 222]   *FEAST DAY: October 14*

A remarkable number of contemporary sources tell the story of St. Callixtus, including the work of the second-century Christian historian Julius Africanus, compiler of the first Christian chronology. Most of the details of Callixtus's disorderly life, however, come from his two bitterest enemies, the Christian theologian and controversialist Tertullian and the antipope Hippolytus. They have left us a scrupulously detailed record of every one of Callixtus's transgressions. The only aspect of his life that Tertullian and Hippolytus shied away from was his conversion.

Around the year 190 in Rome a Christian named Carpophorus set up a bank for his fellow Christians, particularly widows, who needed a safe place to keep their limited funds. Carpophorus had a Christian slave named Callixtus who had experience managing money, so he entrusted the administration of the bank to him. The man couldn't have made a worse choice.

Callixtus's investment decisions were disastrous. Worse still, he had a habit of helping himself to the bank's funds. In short order all the money was gone. Roman Christians who thought they were financially secure suddenly found themselves destitute. As for Callixtus, he ran to the nearest harbor, where he booked passage on the first ship heading out to sea. The destination didn't matter, so long as the ship took him far from his irate master and the Christians he had bankrupted.

But Carpophorus went after his slave. He caught up with Callixtus at the town of Portus, where the runaway slave was aboard a ship anchored in the middle of the harbor, anxiously awaiting a favorable wind. Carpophorus hired a boatman to ferry him out to the vessel. As the little boat drew close, Callixtus recognized the man aboard as his master. In desperation he dove into the sea and tried to swim to safety. By now Carpophorus's boat was within earshot of the ship. He shouted to the sailors not to let Callixtus get away. The crew leapt into their own small boats, fished Callixtus out of the water, and handed him over to Carpophorus.

Under Roman law masters could do whatever they liked with their slaves. Back in Rome Carpophorus sentenced Callixtus to hard labor. The embezzling slave was chained to a gristmill, where he turned the massive stone wheel day after day. It was brutal, exhausting, mind-numbing work. Callixtus, knowing that his master would never forgive him, expected to turn the wheel until he dropped dead in his tracks.

Then rescue came from an unexpected quarter. The ruined depositors from Carpophorus's bank begged him to release Callixtus, arguing that the slave might be persuaded to recover at least some of the money he had squandered. The pleas of his desperate friends touched the heart of Carpophorus; he agreed to free his slave with the understanding that Callixtus would try to regain at least some of the money he had lost.

Callixtus was barely out of his chains when he got into fresh trouble. On Saturday morning he barged into Rome's synagogue, disrupted the Sabbath service, and demanded money from the Jewish congregation. He claimed he was trying get back the funds he had invested with Jewish financiers. This may have been true, but Callixtus should have known better than to disturb religious people at their prayers in order to collect a debt. The brawl that erupted in the synagogue ended with members of the congregation dragging Callixtus into the courtroom of Fuscianus, the prefect of the city.

The Jews charged Callixtus with disturbing the peace

and desecrating a holy place. For good measure, they said they suspected that Callixtus was a member of that outlawed sect known as Christians. By now Carpophorus was in the courtroom, too, and he swore that his slave was no Christian. Technically, of course, Carpophorus was lying since Callixtus had been baptized. But in terms of Callixtus's conduct, no one could describe it as Christlike.

Fuscianus settled the case quickly: the slave Callixtus was to be scourged, then transported to the island of Sardinia to work in the mines.

Turning the gristmill had been bad, but slaving in the mines was a virtual death sentence. The backbreaking labor, the stifling air of the tunnels, the scant food and water allotted to the slaves all but guaranteed that even the strongest man would not survive more than a year. Not that such a massive turnover of prisoners mattered: in the Roman Empire there was never a shortage of slaves.

Back in Rome Carpophorus, the penniless Christians, and the Jews of the city found some satisfaction in the knowledge that the troublesome Callixtus at last was getting what he deserved. But then yet another unforeseen event occurred.

Marcia, the mistress of the emperor Commodus, was a Christian. As Caesar's lover she enjoyed power in her own right, and now she decided to exercise it on behalf of those Christians who had been sentenced to a lingering death in the mines of Sardinia. Marcia asked Pope St. Victor I to prepare a list of these living martyrs so she could arrange for their release. Pope Victor named every Christian prisoner he could think of, but he purposely omitted Callixtus.

Marcia sent an elderly eunuch named Hyacinthus with a letter to the governor of Sardinia asking him, as a personal favor to her, to release the men named on the list. Naturally, the governor was not about to refuse the emperor's mistress.

As Hyacinthus collected all the Christians for the journey home, Callixtus ran forward, dropped to his knees, and, weeping, begged Hyacinthus to take him, too. The old man probably knew Callixtus's reputation, but he could not leave him in the mines to die. And so Callixtus returned to Rome.

Carpophorus was furious to see his slave again, and Pope Victor was horrified that the scoundrel Callixtus was back in the city. Prompted by a mix of prudence and charity, Victor gave Callixtus an allowance and put him up in a house far outside the city walls where, everyone hoped, he could not get into any more trouble.

Time passed, and Callixtus remained quiet. He even showed signs of repentance. Gradually Pope Victor became convinced of the sincerity of Callixtus's conversion. He permitted Callixtus to assist a priest named Zephyrinus who managed the assignment of priests and deacons in Rome.

In 199 Victor died, and Zephyrinus was elected pope. One of the new pope's first acts was to ordain Callixtus a deacon, then put him in charge of a Christian cemetery on the Appian Way. Today that cemetery is known as the Catacomb of St. Callixtus.

By the time Pope Zephyrinus (who would later be canonized as well) died in 217, Callixtus had become so well respected that the clergy and Christian laity of Rome elected the former slave, brawler, and embezzler pope.

Callixtus's brief five-year reign was marked by the virtue he had come to appreciate above all others: mercy. He decreed that Christians who had committed fornication or adultery, even Christians who had fallen into heresy, could be restored to full Communion with the Catholic Church once they had confessed their sins and done penance. Pope Callixtus's ruling split the Church between orthodox Catholics who understood that the Church was in the forgiveness business, and more rigid Catholics who felt that certain sins were unforgivable. The leader of the inflexible faction was Hippolytus, a Roman priest and theologian, who knew about Callixtus's shameful past and despised him for it. An angry, vindictive man, Hippolytus taught that any Christian who committed even a single mortal sin ought to be driven out of the Church and never permitted to return, no matter how sincerely he or she might repent. Callixtus's compassion for penitent sinners enraged Hippolytus. He published an exposé of Callixtus's life. But he didn't stop there: Hippolytus falsely charged

Pope Zephyrinus and Pope Callixtus with holding and teaching heretical ideas about the Blessed Trinity. He described Zephyrinus as an "ignorant and illiterate" dunce whom Callixtus had corrupted with bribes; as for Callixtus, Hippolytus said he was "a man cunning in wickedness, and subtle where deceit was concerned." Hippolytus worked himself into such a fury that he did what no Christian had ever done before: he denied that Callixtus's election was valid and had his followers elect him pope. Hippolytus became the first antipope.

The split between the Catholics faithful to Pope Callixtus and the schismatics who followed Hippolytus was not healed during Callixtus's lifetime. In 222 an anti-Christian mob murdered Callixtus, then threw his body down a well. Christians recovered the martyred pope's remains, burying them in a cemetery outside the city. Today the relics of St. Callixtus are enshrined in Rome's Church of Santa Maria in Trastevere, not far from the place where he was killed. As for Hippolytus, he remained intransigent, insisting that he was the true Bishop of Rome and that the elections of Pope St. Urban I in 222 and Pope St. Pontian in 230 were invalid.

In 235 Emperor Maximinus launched a new persecution of the Church that especially targeted the clergy. Pontian and Hippolytus were among those rounded up. Both were sentenced to a place St. Callixtus had known well—the mines in Sardinia. In that terrible place Hippolytus repented of his schism and asked to be reconciled to the Catholic Church. Soon after, Hippolytus died of the inhuman conditions in the mines. As for Pope Pontian, he was beaten to death by his guards.

Their earthly rivalries and antagonisms resolved at last, Pontian, Hippolytus, and Callixtus became honored as saints and martyrs.

St. Hippolytus, Antipope

[c. 170–c. 236]   *FEAST DAY: August 13*

A few days before Pope John Paul II died, another "pope" passed away in Spain. Clemente Domínguez y Gómez, who called himself Pope Gregory XVII, died March 22, 2005. Domínguez y Gómez believed the Church of Rome was so hopelessly corrupted by Freemasons, Communists, and heretics that he and his followers were the only true Catholics left in the world. In 1978, he proclaimed himself pope.

Domínguez y Gómez was not the only antipope of our time: there is another, living in an undisclosed location, probably somewhere in the western United States. In

1998 a group calling itself the True Catholic Church elected Father Lucian Pulvermacher, O.F.M. Cap., pope. The conclave was held in a remote cabin in Montana. Since most of the electors—all lay men and women—could not make the journey to such an isolated location, they phoned in their votes. Father Pulvermacher took the name Pius XIII.

As antipopes go, Gregory XVII and Pius XIII have been harmless. Farcical, certainly, and a little sad, but since their influence doesn't extend beyond a handful of oddballs they do no injury to the Catholic Church or to society at large. During the Middle Ages it was a different story.

Between 1058 and 1449 twenty-two antipopes afflicted the Church. Unlike the eccentrics who claim to be pope today, the medieval antipopes were ambitious, unprincipled men whose grab for power caused disruption throughout the Catholic world. The worst was the Great Schism, a traumatic period that dragged on from 1378 until 1419, when there were two, and then between 1406 and 1417 three, rival popes. The situation was so confusing even saints had a hard time determining who was the legitimate Holy Father: St. Catherine of Siena backed one contender, while St. Vincent Ferrer backed another.

On a day-to-day basis the antipopes' effect on the Church proved disastrous. Rival popes created rival colleges of cardinals; each insisted that papal revenues belonged to them. When a diocese needed a new bishop, or a monastery a new abbot, each pope made an appointment, so two or three men showed up at a cathedral or an abbey, each claiming that the office belonged to him.

And then there were the spiritual issues. In theological debates the pope declared what was true doctrine and what was heresy. The spiritual authority of bishops and archbishops came through him. He disciplined wayward priests and princes, granted indulgences, canonized saints, and approved new religious orders. But only a legitimate pope could exercise such authority. In the next world, what would happen to Catholics who gave their allegiance to the wrong pope? It was a question that tormented consciences in every corner of Christendom.

Given the disgrace to the Church and what was at stake for the ordinary Catholic, it comes as a shock to learn that the first antipope appeared in 217. His name was Hippolytus, the most brilliant theologian in Rome, a man of limitless ego, a rigorist who did not know the meaning of the words "compassion" or "forgiveness." Faults and foibles aside, Hippolytus enjoyed a wide-ranging reputation as a man who grasped subtle distinctions in any theological argument. About the year 212 when Origen, the most learned Christian theologian of the time, traveled to Rome from his home in Egypt, he made a point of going to hear Hippolytus preach.

Hippolytus began his slide into schism during the reign of Pope St. Zephyrinus (reigned 198/9–217). In one of his books, *Philosophymena*, Hippolytus writes off Zephyrinus as a man of no education. Compared to Hippolytus, the new pope probably was a mediocre scholar. Certainly he could not follow Hippolytus's complex theories on the relationship between God the Father and God the Son, nor did he try. Zephyrinus affirmed, in simple terms, what the Church had always taught: that there was one God in three Divine Persons, the Father, the Son, and the Holy Spirit. More intense theological speculation of the type Hippolytus enjoyed did not interest the pope—as long as it was not heresy.

But Zephyrinus the dullard pope was not the only person troubling Hippolytus. He had an irrational hatred for Callixtus, a former slave, embezzler, and troublemaker who had repented and been appointed by Zephyrinus as supervisor of the Christian cemeteries outside Rome. (St. Callixtus's story is told in detail in the preceding chapter.) When Zephyrinus died in 217, the Roman clergy elected Callixtus pope. This was too much for Hippolytus. He believed that he should have been elected. As he nursed his grudge, he convinced himself and others that Callixtus held unorthodox opinions about the nature of Jesus Christ, and that he was corrupting the Church by absolving penitent adulterers and fornicators and readmitting to the Church heartbroken Christians who, out of fear of torture and death, had caved under the pressure of the Roman authorities and denied their faith. With the backing of other anti-Callixtus Christians in Rome, Hippolytus severed his ties to the Church and permitted his followers to elect him pope.

Five years later a pagan mob attacked and murdered Callixtus in the streets of Rome's Trastevere neighborhood. Yet Hippolytus did not relinquish his claim to the papacy. The orthodox Roman clergy elected St. Urban I pope. During this peaceful reign (Urban is one of the few early popes not to have died a martyr) Hippolytus still adamantly refused to return to the Church. In 230 St. Pontian was elected pope, and five years later Rome got a new emperor, Maximinus. Almost immediately the emperor launched a new persecution of Christians, taking special care to target the leaders of the Church. Pope Pontian and the antipope Hippolytus were both seized in the roundup and deported to the mines in Sardinia. For the sake of the Church, Pontian resigned the papacy so a new pope could be elected. This act of selfless concern for the good of the Church appears to have pricked Hippolytus's conscience. In Sardinia he repented his schism and begged Pontian to reconcile him to the Church.

Within a few months of Pontian's resignation and Hippolytus's repentance, both men died of the harsh treatment they suffered in the mines. Pope St. Fabian (reigned 236–250) arranged for the bodies of the two martyrs to be brought back and buried in Rome, where the Christians of the city accepted the onetime anti-pope's repentance, forgave him his schism, and venerated him as a saint—thus showing themselves to be more like Callixtus than Hippolytus.

St. Christopher,
Servant of the Devil

[Died c. 250] FEAST DAY: *July 25*

Poor St. Christopher. For centuries he was one of the popular saints, yet today most Catholics believe one of two things about the patron saint of travelers: the pope expelled St. Christopher from the calendar of saints because he never existed, or the pope demoted St. Christopher and he is no longer a saint (in which case maybe we should call him "Mr. Christopher"). The de-sainting of St. Christopher has become a religious urban legend, a story that "everyone knows is true" but in fact is flat-out wrong.

St. Christopher is still a saint in good standing. There is no doubt among hagiographers—the scholars who study saints professionally—that there was an early martyr named Christopher.

What, then, is the source of the misinformation about St. Christopher? It began in 1969 when Pope Paul VI authorized a complete revision of the Church's liturgical calendar. Some popular saints such as St. Ursula and St. Catherine of Alexandria were removed from the calendar because Vatican hagiographers believed they were apocryphal characters. Other saints had their feast days lowered in rank to an optional memorial, which lets local churches decide if they will commemorate the saint in the Mass of the day. Media reports at the time of the shake-up often got the facts wrong, only adding to the confusion. It didn't help that many bishops and parish priests failed to explain to the people in the pews what was happening. Unfortunately, St. Christopher was one of the victims of this mess.

There are perhaps as many as forty thousand saints recognized by the Catholic Church. But there are only 365 days in a year. Consequently, every day is the feast day of dozens of saints. Since time immemorial July 25 has been the feast day of both the apostle St. James the Greater and of St. Christopher (to say nothing of many other less well-known saints). In the hierarchy of saints, an apostle outranks a martyr, even a martyr as famous as St. Christopher. After the 1969 revision of the Church's calendar, priests throughout the world were instructed to offer Mass on July 25 in honor of St.

James. This is the general rule, but it is not carved in stone. Parishes and chapels dedicated to St. Christopher, or regions where St. Christopher is especially honored, have the option of celebrating his Mass on July 25.

There was a real St. Christopher. The Roman Martyrology, the ancient compendium of Christians who were martyred during the first centuries of the Church, records Christopher's martyrdom in Lycia, in present-day Turkey, during the persecution of the emperor Decius (reigned 249–251). The executioners shot Christopher through with arrows, then beheaded him. Devotion to St. Christopher spread quickly in both the East and the West: churches were being dedicated to him as early as 452, while the earliest surviving image of St. Christopher, preserved in the Monastery of St. Catherine on Mount Sinai, dates from about the year 550.

Those are the facts. What follows is the legend.

At birth the man we know as Christopher was named Reprobus, which comes from the Latin word for someone destined for damnation. When he reached manhood Reprobus was tall, almost a giant, and exceptionally strong. His massive physique made him vain, and he swore he would serve only the greatest power on earth. The king of Canaan had a mighty army and ruled over a vast territory. When Reprobus offered to serve him, the king accepted at once and made Reprobus part of his inner circle.

One day the king's fool was singing a song that made frequent mention of the devil. Every time Satan's name was mentioned, the king, who was a Christian, made the sign of the cross. "Why do you do that?" Reprobus asked. "I make this sign," the king answered, "to ward off the devil so he will do me no harm."

"If you are afraid of the devil," Reprobus said, "then I will go serve him, because I will serve no one except the most powerful lord in the world."

Out in the desert Reprobus encountered an army of fierce-looking men. Their commander, who looked more terrible than the rest, asked, "What are you doing in this wasteland?"

"I am searching for the devil," Reprobus replied. "I hear that he is the greatest lord in the world."

"I am the one you are looking for," the leader said. "I am the devil."

So Reprobus swore eternal allegiance to Satan.

One day as the devil and his men were marching along, a roadside cross came into view. Trembling, the devil ordered his men to leave the road and led them on a long detour through rough and rocky country.

"What was that all about?" Reprobus asked.

"There was a man named Christ who was nailed to a cross," the devil answered. "Every time I see a cross, I think of Christ and I am afraid."

"Then Christ must be stronger than you," Reprobus said. "I will go serve him."

After a long period of wandering, Reprobus met a Christian hermit who explained the kind of service Christ required.

"You will have to fast in penance for your sinful life," the hermit said.

"I can't do that," Reprobus said. "My appetite is too great. Let the Lord Christ require something else from me."

"Then spend your days in prayer," the hermit said.

"I don't know any prayers," Reprobus answered. "Give me some other task to perform."

The hermit thought for a moment before he spoke again. Nearby was a river. The water was deep and the current so strong that many travelers who tried to cross it were drowned. "You are tall and strong," the hermit said. "Go live beside the river and carry on your shoulders anyone who wants to cross. That will please Christ, and perhaps he will show himself to you there."

"This I can do," Reprobus said. So the hermit baptized Reprobus, giving him the new name Christopher, which means "Christ-bearer," and sent him on his way. Near the riverbank Christopher built himself a hut. In the woods he found a tall, stout staff to steady himself when he carried travelers across the river.

One day, while resting in his hut, he heard a child's voice crying, "Christopher, come out and carry me across."

Outside the hut Christopher found a little boy. He

grabbed his staff, lifted the child to his shoulder, and stepped into the water. As Christopher made his way through the river, the current grew rougher, the waves higher, and the boy became heavier and heavier. Christopher feared he would lose his step, that both he and the little boy would be swept away and drowned. At last, exhausted and gasping for breath, he reached the safety of the opposite shore.

"Boy," Christopher said, "you put us both in great danger. Who are you?"

The little boy answered, "Today you carried on your shoulders the Creator of the world. I am Christ your king." Then the Christ Child vanished.

St. Pelagia, Promiscuous Actress

[5th century?]   FEAST DAY: October 8

For the story of St. Pelagia we have two primary sources. The first is an entirely reliable account of the conversion of a notorious actress related by St. John Chrysostom in his Sermon 67 on St. Matthew's gospel. There is one problem with St. John's sermon—he never mentions the actress's name. The second source is a detailed life of St. Pelagia written by a man who calls himself James the Deacon and claims to have known her. There is also a problem with James's story: it is almost certainly a work of fiction.

Providing full-scale biographies for obscure saints

was a minor industry in the early centuries of the Church. The discovery of the tomb of a previously unknown martyr or a passing reference in some document to a local holy man or woman was all it took to fire up the imaginations of storytellers. And the phenomenon continues. In 1802 archaeologists excavating in Rome's Catacomb of St. Priscilla discovered the bones of a young woman named Philomena. Carved into the tomb slab were images of a scourge, three arrows, a palm frond, and a lily—the emblems of martyrdom and of virginity—along with an anchor, the symbol of hope. The find created a sensation in the Catholic world, and almost immediately the young woman was being invoked by the faithful as St. Philomena.

If ever there was an account of Philomena's life, it has not come down to us. In fact, her name does not even appear on any of the ancient lists of Roman martyrs. But the devotees of St. Philomena did not have to wait long to learn all about their saint: in 1863 an Italian nun, Mother Mary Louisa of Jesus, claimed to have had a vision of St. Philomena during which the young martyr told her story. This "biography" is still in print today.

To return to St. Pelagia, St. John Chrysostom tells us she was an actress from Phoenicia whose reputation as a great lady of the stage and as a woman of notoriously easy virtue extended throughout Asia Minor. Her theatrical performances must have been especially lurid since St. John says, "Nothing was more vile than she was, when she was on the stage." The men she took as her lovers became intoxicated with her. For Pelagia's sake fathers abandoned their children, wealthy men squandered their estates. She even seduced the empress's brother. Trying to account for Pelagia's power over men, St. John wondered if she drugged them, and speculated that perhaps she used sorcery.

Then, inexplicably, grace came to Pelagia. She repented. She asked to be baptized. She entered a convent and lived the life of a saint until the day she died. That is all that we know for certain about the anonymous penitent that we call St. Pelagia.

James the Deacon's version may not be anywhere near as reliable as St. John's, but it is a good read. He began in Antioch, where eight bishops had gathered. It was a fine day, and they were all sitting outside the doors of a church, listening to a homily from St. Nonnus, bishop of Heliopolis. Suddenly down the street came a crowd of handsome young men and lovely young women, all splendidly dressed, and following a woman of ravishing beauty. The modest ladies of Antioch wore a veil in public, but this woman went through the streets with her head uncovered and her shoulders bare. The bishops lowered their eyes and turned their faces away from the lascivious sight. But Bishop Nonnus watched her until she was lost in the crowd.

Turning back to his brother bishops he said, "Did

not the wonderful beauty of that woman delight you?" The bishops didn't answer, embarrassed that the good old man had forgotten himself. So Nonnus repeated his question, "Did not her beauty delight you?" Still the bishops kept quiet. By now they must have been wondering if Nonnus had lost his self-control.

"How many hours did that woman spend washing, dressing, and adorning herself, then studying herself in the mirror to make certain that everything about her was perfect before she went out in public to show herself to her admirers?" Nonnus said. "We never spend so much effort to adorn our souls, to wash them with repentance and clothe them with the virtues so that we might appear pleasing to God."

It was a clever sermon. Nonnus used an unexpected encounter with a shameless sinner prancing through the streets to teach his brother bishops a lesson in holiness.

Back in his room after the meeting had ended, Nonnus prayed for Pelagia, "O Lord, do not permit such beauty to remain a slave to demons."

The following Sunday Bishop Nonnus was preaching in Antioch's cathedral when Pelagia happened to be walking by. On impulse, she stepped inside the church. As Nonnus spoke about the mercy of God Pelagia began to reflect on her life; she was so filled with self-loathing and sorrow that she wept uncontrollably. As the congregation filed out of the cathedral, Pelagia sought out Bishop Nonnus and begged him to make her a Christian.

The bishop heard her confession, gave her a concise instruction in the faith, and then baptized her. To celebrate Pelagia's conversion, Nonnus invited the visiting bishops to a banquet. Afterward the bishop found her a room at the house of a pious Christian matron named Romana.

That night the devil woke Pelagia. "What evil have I ever done to you?" he asked. "Tell me how I have offended, and I will give you whatever you want. Only do not leave me. Do not make me a laughingstock." Pelagia made the sign of the cross and drove the devil away.

Pelagia was wealthy. Now she freed her slaves, giving each of them gold and silver so they could begin new lives. Then she handed over the balance of her wealth to Bishop Nonnus for the relief of the poor and the suffering. One night she cropped her hair short, put on a tattered monk's robe, and slipped out of Romana's house.

Pelagia walked from Antioch to Jerusalem, where she lived as a hermit on the Mount of Olives. Because she was young and attractive and had no beard, the people of Jerusalem took her for a eunuch. Pelagia never corrected them.

Years later Nonnus's deacon, James, went on pilgrimage to the Holy Land. In Jerusalem he heard about a pious hermit who lived on the Mount of Olives. When he reached the holy man's cell, he was surprised to hear the hermit greet him by name.

A few days later, while James was still in Jerusalem,

the hermit died. He joined the monks who went to prepare the hermit's body for burial. When they stripped the body to wash it, the monks were astonished to see that the holy man was a woman. Only then did James recognize the hermit as Pelagia.

St. Genesius, Scoffer

[*Died c. 300*]   FEAST DAY: *August 25*

Well into the twentieth century actors were regarded as immoral riffraff: it is a prejudice that goes back to ancient Rome. The Greeks respected actors as artists, but the Romans had nothing but contempt for stage performers. That most actors were prisoners captured in war, or slaves, or at least foreigners only confirmed the Romans in their negative opinion. Under Roman law actors were not permitted to vote and barred from joining the army. Since everyone believed they were bad, many actors took the easy way and behaved badly.

Under the emperors the classic Greek and Roman comedies and tragedies always found an audience, but perhaps the most popular form of entertainment in the theaters was mime. Most mime plays were bawdy stories of unfaithful wives and husbands, acted out with plenty of lewd gestures. There was another reason why mime was popular: unlike the standard theater fare in which men played all the parts, mime featured both actors and actresses. Invariably at some point in the mime the actresses would appear on stage naked.

During the first century of the Christian era, producers of mime concocted a new way to draw a crowd by introducing into the performances actual executions. In the final scene of a play called *Laureolus* the actor who had been cast as the title character was replaced by a condemned criminal who was tortured to death, onstage, in full view of the excited audience. The same refinement was introduced in the mimed account of Prometheus, the Titan who stole fire from the gods and was punished by being fettered to a rock. At the end of the play a condemned man dressed as Prometheus was dragged out from the wings and nailed, hand and foot, to a piece of stage scenery.

Genesius was a comic actor during the reign of Diocletian, the emperor who was intent upon eliminating the Christians from the empire once and for all. When Genesius's theatrical troupe was commanded to perform before Diocletian, they decided to prepare a play that would be topical: they wrote a new farce that mocked the Christian sacrament of baptism.

Genesius was cast as the convert to be baptized. But at the climactic moment, as the water was poured over his head and the actor playing the priest spoke the words of the baptismal rite, something remarkable happened. Divine grace flowed over Genesius just as if his baptism had been authentic. He scrapped the sacrilegious lines he was supposed to recite, and instead looked Diocletian in the eye as he ad-libbed a speech denouncing the emperor for his cruelty to the Christians.

At first Diocletian thought the speech was only a bold joke, in keeping with the parody. But as Genesius continued to defend the Christians and condemn the persecution, Diocletian understood that the brazen actor was castigating him in public, in front of his own guests. The emperor stopped the performance, ordered Genesius arrested, and condemned him to be tortured to death.

Genesius was probably hauled off to prison and tortured there. But given the Romans' tolerance of gruesome spectacles onstage, it's possible that he met his death in front of an appreciative if sadistic audience, either in an arena or one of Rome's theaters.

The executioners tore Genesius's sides with iron hooks and burned him with torches, all the while urging him to deny he was a Christian and save his life. But

Genesius, perhaps as astonished as anyone by his conversion, remained firm. "Were I to be killed a thousand times for my allegiance to Christ," he said, "I would still go on as I have begun." Death was a long time coming to Genesius, yet in his agony he repented of "sneering at the Holy Name in holy men, and coming so late to worship the true king."

St. Genesius is the patron saint of actors, and devotion to him is strong in the theatrical community. One example: in St. Malachy's Church, the parish in New York City's Broadway theater district, there is a side chapel dedicated to the martyred actor.

St. Genesius's relics are enshrined in the Church of Santa Susanna, the parish of the American community in Rome.

St. Moses the Ethiopian, Cutthroat and Gang Leader

[c. 330–c. 405]   FEAST DAY: *August 28*

Moses began life as a slave in the home of an Egyptian government official. Tall, powerfully built, and with a ferocious expression on his face, he must have been an intimidating presence around the house. When his master discovered that Moses had been stealing from him, he drove him out.

The desert of Egypt at this time attracted two types of men: monks and brigands. Moses, a lustful, vengeful, violent man, took up a life of crime, becoming the leader of a gang of seventy-five men who were almost as wicked as he. Moses and his brigands became the terror of the Egyptian desert, raiding villages, robbing and sometimes killing travelers who made the mistake of trying to cross the band's territory. The governor of the province sent out troops to capture or kill Moses and his gang, but the bandits defeated and drove off every squad sent against them.

One night, as Moses and his gang were creeping up on an especially rich victim, sheepdogs began to bark, spoiling the surprise and forcing the thieves to retreat into the darkness. Moses swore to track down and kill the shepherd whose dogs had ruined his scheme. In time he learned that the offending shepherd had moved his flock to the opposite side of the Nile. The river was flooded and about a mile wide at that time of the year, but Moses stripped off his shirt, put his short sword between his teeth, and swam to the shepherd's camp. When the poor man saw the brigand chief wading out of the river, he hid himself by burrowing into the sand.

Moses, enraged that the shepherd had gotten away, slaughtered the four best rams in the flock, tied them together, then swam back across the Nile with the carcasses in tow. He ate the best parts of the rams, threw away the rest of the meat, and exchanged the skins for a large quantity of wine—all of which he drank before setting out on a fifty-mile hike back to his own camp.

The day came at last when the governor sent a force strong enough to destroy the brigands. Faced with such a large body of troops, the robbers scattered. Moses traveled alone through the desert until he reached the monastery of Petra in Skete, one of Egypt's most renowned monastic communities. The monks here were anchorites, which means they lived like hermits, each in his own small hut called a cell; they only came together as a community for religious services on Saturday and Sunday. In Moses' mind, this was the perfect hideout. He would hole up with the monks until the situation in the desert settled down, then go back and round up whatever remained of his band.

One look at this crude giant of a man, and the monks must have known he was not some pilgrim. Nevertheless, they gave Moses a cell, fed him, treated him kindly, and asked him no questions. As time passed, however, something unexpected began to happen to Moses. The monks' goodness transformed him. He no longer wanted to return to his life as a robber and murderer; he wanted to start a new life at Petra.

It wasn't easy. Moses found chastity especially difficult. He had slept with a lot of women, and to stop suddenly, to vow to remain chaste for the rest of his life, seemed impossible. The temptations he felt were so strong he almost abandoned the life of a monk, but the abbot St. Isidore reassured him. "Do not be grieved," the holy man said. "This is only the beginning. That is why the demons have attacked you so vehemently, trying to force you back into your old habits. But if you endure, the demons will get discouraged and leave you alone."

Moses increased the intensity of his prayers and fasted more than the rule of the monastery recommended. He had better control of his body, but asleep at night he could not control his dreams. Back he went to St. Isidore. "You have not kept your mind from imagining these things," the abbot said. "That is why you have these dreams."

But an active libido was not Moses' only trial. Whenever he was challenged, whenever he felt threatened, he had lashed out violently—and usually that had settled the problem. Now he made a private vow never to harm another human being. When four brigands made the mistake of attacking him, Moses overpowered them, tied them together, slung the four over his shoulder, and carried them to the monastery church, where he dumped them on the floor. "I cannot hurt anyone," he told the astonished monks. "What do you want to do with them?"

Guided by St. Isidore, Moses learned to overcome his sinful impulses. Once, just before dawn, Isidore and Moses climbed to the roof of the monastery to watch the sun rise. "See how long it takes for the light to drive away the darkness of night?" Isidore said. "It is the same with the soul."

Moses was seventy-five years old when a warning

reached the monks that an army of Berbers was heading for the monastery. Some of the monks wanted to fight, but Moses convinced them it was better to flee into the desert rather than shed blood. As for Moses, he and seven companion monks stayed behind. As the Berbers rampaged through the monastery they found Moses and his brothers, and killed them all.

St. Fabiola, Bigamist

[Died 399]   FEAST DAY: *December 27*

Statues of 140 saints stand along the edge of the great colonnade that embraces St. Peter's Square in Rome. Unrecognized in this crowd is a statue of St. Fabiola, a woman few Christians have even heard of. Fabiola, once notorious as a public sinner, and then illustrious as one of the most charitable Christians in Rome, has been lost in the crowd of thousands upon thousands of saints who have come after her.

She might have slipped our notice completely were it not for St. Jerome, who knew Fabiola and wrote her eulogy.

Fabiola was a Christian and a patrician. No doubt her husband came from a distinguished family as well, but we do not know if he was a Christian. We do not even know his name. We do know that he made Fabiola miserable, cheating on her on an epic scale. Jerome says the man's adulteries were so numerous, so flagrant "not even a prostitute or a common slave could have put up with them."

There came a point when Fabiola would tolerate it no longer. She divorced her husband.

While a Catholic may separate from a spouse, he or she is forbidden to divorce and remarry. Christ himself forbade it in St. Matthew's gospel, yet Fabiola defied this law. She was still a young woman. She found it too hard to live without the company of a man, so she obtained a civil divorce from her first husband and, in a civil ceremony, married another, better man.

The Church could not recognize Fabiola's divorce or her civil marriage. Her actions, although understandable, placed Fabiola in the category of a persistent sinner and barred her from receiving the sacraments. For a prominent Christian patrician to flout the laws of the Church caused a public scandal.

Then the unexpected happened: Fabiola's second husband died. She had already placed herself outside the Church; she could have married for a third time if she wanted. But grace touched Fabiola's heart. One Sunday she appeared among the penitents outside

Rome's Lateran Basilica, the church that is the pope's cathedral. In the fourth century repentance and absolution were much more public than they are today. Sinners did not slip into a private confessional; they came to Sunday Mass dressed in miserable clothes, unwashed and unkempt, so everyone in the congregation would know that they repented the wickedness they had done. St. Jerome describes the scene, saying noble Fabiola appeared before the throng of Christians with "disheveled hair, pale features, soiled hands and unwashed neck." That Sunday, the pope absolved her of her sins.

Now that she was restored to the Church, Fabiola devoted herself to good works. She sold her jewels, her land, everything she owned. With the money from the sale of her property she opened the first hospital in the West, nursing, washing, and feeding the patients herself. Her wealth was so extensive, however, that Fabiola could expand her work, endowing monasteries and convents, clothing the poor of Rome, and supporting invalids.

With her hospital up and running, Fabiola decided to make a pilgrimage to the Holy Land. That is how she met St. Jerome: he had settled in Bethlehem, where he was working on the authoritative Latin translation of the Bible that has come to be called the Vulgate. Fabiola charmed Jerome, who could be thin-skinned, cantankerous, and difficult to get along with. She lingered in Bethlehem, and they became good friends. Jerome thought Fabiola might stay in the Holy Land permanently, but when the Huns invaded Syria and Palestine, Fabiola fled back to Rome. Soon afterward she died.

Her funeral was more like an old Roman triumph for a conquering hero than a requiem. The churches were thronged with mourners praying for her soul, and as her body was carried through Rome to its tomb, "the streets, porches, and roofs from which a view could be obtained were inadequate to accommodate the spectators." Her friend St. Jerome wrote what could be her epitaph, "Where sin hath abounded, grace hath much more abounded."

St. Augustine, Heretic and Playboy

[354–430] FEAST DAY: August 28

At the risk of stating the obvious, St. Augustine's *Confessions* is a remarkable book. It is the world's first autobiography. It provides a snapshot of life in the Roman Empire just before the fall of Rome. And it offers readers a detailed portrait of a well-to-do family.

Augustine was born in the rural town of Thagaste, now Souk Ahras in Algeria. His mother, Monica, was a Catholic and a Berber (one of the country's native people). His father, Patricius, was a pagan, a Roman citizen, and a member of Thagaste's town council. Monica and Patricius were not aristocrats, but they derived enough income from their property that Patricius never had to hold down a job.

Like the rest of the Roman Empire at this time, North Africa was religiously diverse. In 315 the emperor Constantine bestowed his favor on the Catholic Church. He gave the Lateran Palace to the pope as his residence. He funded the construction of churches throughout Rome—including St. Peter's—and extended his church-building program to the Holy Land. In spite of the imperial preference for Catholicism, other forms of worship hung on. Roman paganism, local forms of paganism (Monica's name was derived from that of the Carthaginian goddess Mon), a host of cults, various strains of Christianity, and of course Judaism all existed side by side.

Patricius appears to have been religiously indifferent, but he did not interfere with Monica's religious life, even permitting her to raise their children as Catholics. When Augustine was born Monica had a priest anoint him with holy oil, forming the shape of a cross, and sprinkle blessed salt, a rite of exorcism, on his tongue. But she did not ask for her boy to be baptized. This was not uncommon in the first centuries of the Church. Since baptism washes away all sin, many men and women who lived and worshipped as Christians all their lives put off the sacrament until they were on their deathbeds, when it would virtually guarantee that their souls would go straight to Heaven.

In addition to Augustine, Monica and Patricius had another son, Navigius, and a daughter whose name may have been Perpetua. But Augustine was his mother's favorite. New mothers of Monica's social class gave their infants to a slave to nurse, but Monica insisted on breast-feeding her child herself. She liked to have her boy with her, "as is the way with mothers," Augustine recalled, "but far more than most mothers."

Patricius loved Augustine, and was ambitious for him. He wanted his boy to have a fine education, to enter a distinguished and lucrative profession, to make a good marriage and have a large family. Once, when Augustine was sixteen, father and son went to the baths. As young Augustine undressed, his father saw body hair and realized that his son had reached puberty. That night Patricius forgot all about universities and professions as he indulged in dreams of his future grandchildren. In celebration of Augustine's budding virility, Patricius got drunk.

Monica, however, was more single-minded. If Augustine married and started a family now, he would never get an education or have any chance at a career. Monica realized that not marrying him off was risky: he might visit prostitutes, acquire a mistress, or chase other men's wives. In the end Monica decided in favor of more education for her son, but she warned him against committing sexual sins, especially the sin of adultery. Augustine says he treated her "womanish advice" with contempt. He was, as he says in his *Confessions*, "in the mood to be seduced."

In 371, at age seventeen, Augustine went to Carthage to attend the great university there. He had barely arrived when he did find a mistress and they moved in together. A year later the woman (in none of his writings does Augustine ever mention her name) gave birth to a son they named Adeodatus, which means "gift from God."

This was exactly what Monica had feared, but there was worse news coming. In Carthage Augustine joined the Manicheans, a sect that liked to regard its members as a spiritual elite. The Manicheans believed that two constantly warring powers dominated the universe: the Father of Greatness was the source of all positive, immaterial qualities such as light and intelligence; the other power, generally called Satan, ruled over the base material world and was the source of everything evil. In the course of history many "Jesuses" had come to earth to assist humankind in its struggle against evil, but none of these Jesus figures had ever triumphed over Satan. Catholics at the time were divided over whether Manicheism was a form of paganism or an especially foul heresy. Monica didn't worry about nice distinctions. On Augustine's first visit home after he became a Manichean, his outraged mother barred the door and refused to let him in the house.

Patricius had died in 371. Now it seemed to Monica that she had lost her son, too. Heartbroken, she went to see a bishop who had once been a Manichean himself. Monica felt if anyone could point out to Augustine his folly, it was this man. But the bishop said argument would be futile at this stage when Augustine was in the first flush of his conversion. This was not the answer Monica wanted to hear. She wept; she pleaded; she made such a nuisance of herself that the bishop lost his temper. "Go away from me!" he cried. But almost at once he regained his composure, and offered Monica a little comfort. "Don't worry. It is not possible that the son of so many tears should be lost forever."

Heaven, too, stepped in to console Monica. One night she dreamt she was standing on a narrow wooden beam with a handsome, radiant young man. The youth told her to dry her tears because someday her son would be with her. When she told Augustine her dream he said they could indeed be together if she joined the Manicheans. Monica, who always had a quick tongue, replied, "He didn't say I was to be with you. He said you were to be with me!"

In 383 Augustine decided to go to Rome to look for a position teaching philosophy. He would take his mistress and Adeodatus, of course, but he did not want his mother along. Rather than tell Monica, Augustine did something very cruel. On the day of departure the family went to the harbor, where Augustine suggested Monica visit a small dockside chapel dedicated to the martyr St. Cyprian. While his mother prayed, Augustine boarded the ship and sailed without her. By the time Monica came out of the chapel Augustine's ship was out of sight. She stood alone on the dock, beside herself with grief.

The mean-spirited trick Augustine played on Monica kept mother and son estranged for two years. And there is a certain visceral satisfaction in learning that Augustine failed to make his fortune or his reputation as a teacher in Rome. So with his mistress and Adeodatus Augustine moved again, this time to Milan, where the emperor held court, and where it was said intellectuals were welcomed. Monica moved to Milan, too, and there she and Augustine reconciled.

In Milan Monica attended Mass at the cathedral, where she heard the city's bishop, St. Ambrose, preach. Intellectually Ambrose was on par with Augustine. He had been trained in the classics, and he was a polished, eloquent orator. And he had courage. Emperor Theodosius had ordered Ambrose to turn over a Catholic church to the Arian heretics. Ambrose refused. During Holy Week, 386, the emperor sent troops to surround Ambrose's cathedral and demand that he give up one of his churches to the Arians. Once again Ambrose refused. Then the bishop and his congregation (Monica was in the throng that day) barricaded themselves inside the church and waited to see what the emperor would do. On Holy Thursday Theodosius backed down, called off his troops, and left the Catholics of Milan unmolested with their churches undisturbed.

Augustine was impressed by the way the bishop had conducted himself during his moral showdown with the emperor. He began accompanying his mother to Mass to hear Ambrose preach.

Then one day as he was reading the *Academia* by Cicero, his favorite classical author, Augustine ran across a passage in which Cicero derided the folly of otherwise intelligent men who let themselves be beguiled by some oddball sect. Manicheism could not withstand the one-two punch of Ambrose and Cicero. Like Theodosius, Augustine capitulated; he began to take religious instruction from Ambrose.

It fell to Monica to tell her son something he would not like to hear. As a Catholic he could not continue to live in sin with his mistress. As a gentleman, he could not marry her because she was of low birth. Augustine would have to send away the woman he had lived with for seventeen years. Augustine said giving her up "cut and wounded" his heart. She went back to North Africa, but Adeodatus stayed with Augustine.

Years earlier a testy African bishop had promised Monica that her son would not be lost. That prediction was fulfilled at last on the night of April 24–25, 387, at the Mass of the Easter Vigil, when St. Ambrose baptized Augustine and Adeodatus. It was the crowning moment of Monica's life. A few weeks later she fell suddenly ill. As she lay dying she told Augustine not to worry that she could not be buried beside his father in Africa. "Lay this body anywhere," she said, "do not worry about this: I have only one request, that wherever you are you remember me at the altar of the Lord."

Monica was making a prediction of her own, that Augustine would enter the priesthood. He did, of course, going on to be consecrated a bishop, and creating a body of work that earned him a reputation as the greatest theologian the Church has ever known, second in influence only to the apostle St. Paul. No one could have foreseen all this years earlier when Augustine went off to college, eager for sexual exploits. And it all came to pass thanks to his mother's prayers.

St. Alipius, Obsessed
with Blood Sports

[c. 360–c. 429]   *FEAST DAY: August 15*

Shows and spectacles were essential to Roman life. Under the Caesars, before Christianity dominated the empire, fully half the days of the year were public holidays celebrated with races, wild animal hunts, and gladiatorial combats. Every city in the empire had an arena, and Carthage, as the leading city in Roman North Africa, had one that was especially impressive. It was here that Alipius spent an inordinate amount of his time as a young man.

He was born in Thagaste, St. Augustine's hometown, the son of a noble family. His parents sent him to the university in Carthage where Augustine was teaching. There, Alipius became one of Augustine's students, and eventually a close friend. After growing up in a backwater such as Thagaste, Alipius was dazzled by Carthage. The one place in town that captivated him above all the rest was not Augustine's lecture hall, but the arena. Alipius became addicted to what Augustine characterized in his *Confessions* as "the folly of the circus games."

When a Roman referred to the circus he meant chariot races. The races drew fanatical crowds who lived and died by the success of their favorite teams, their favorite charioteers. Nor did the fans limit themselves to strenuous cheering: gambling was endemic at the races. It was not unusual for a man to bankrupt himself in a single day of betting. And if the thrill of the races and the excitement of placing daring wagers didn't offer enough stimulation, there were plenty of prostitutes working the crowd.

Augustine thought it disgraceful that a young man as intellectually promising as Alipius should waste his time in such degrading company. One day in class, while explaining a philosophical point, Augustine saw an opportunity to illustrate his argument with an analogy to the races. Augustine recalled in his *Confessions* that he was "bitingly sarcastic" about people who were addicted to such vulgar entertainment. The words struck home. Alipius, Augustine tells us, "gave his mind a shaking, and all the filth of the circus games dropped away from him, and he stopped going to them."

But Alipius's conversion was short-lived. From Carthage he went to Rome to study law. One day after dinner he met some friends in the street. They were on their way to the amphitheater to see the gladiators. Alipius declined to join them, saying he was a changed man, that even if they dragged him to the amphitheater he would shut his eyes and think of something ennobling. "I shall be as one not there," he said. To test Alipius's resolve, his friends did indeed drag him to the amphitheater, seating him amidst a mob of frenzied spectators. True to his word, Alipius kept his eyes shut and forced his mind to think of something other than what was going on all around him. But a great roar from the crowd broke his concentration; out of curiosity, Alipius opened his eyes. One of the gladiators had fallen to the ground, wounded by his opponent. The sight of the fighter's blood dripping into the sand, the deafening sound of the various factions in the stands calling for the death blow, or crying for mercy, or urging the fallen gladiator to get up and fight on, intoxicated Alipius. "His eyes were riveted," Augustine says. "He imbibed madness." Before he knew what he was doing Alipius was on his feet, screaming himself hoarse with the rest of the spectators.

Alipius's old habit was nothing compared to his newly acquired taste for blood. He returned so often that the friends who had first taken him to the games got tired of going, so Alipius sought out other fans of the amphitheater and went with them. Soon he was coaxing other men, as innocent as he had once been, to come along to see the gladiators fight. Alipius's bloodlust was all consuming, and this time there was nothing Augustine could say to dissuade his friend.

But where St. Augustine failed, St. Ambrose, the bishop of Milan, succeeded. In 384 Augustine moved to Milan to teach philosophy; Alipius, now a lawyer, went with him. In Carthage both men had joined the Manicheans, a sect whose members considered themselves a spiritual and intellectual elite. Manicheans believed in two gods or powers, one good, the other evil, who were locked in an eternal struggle for dominance over the universe. Few Catholic bishops at the time could impress Augustine and Alipius, but Ambrose had received a classical education, and he had a gift for oratory that attracted crowds to any church where he was scheduled to preach.

Drawn by Ambrose's reputation for eloquence, Augustine began attending the bishop's Masses. And where Augustine went, Alipius followed. Ambrose's sermons fell on fertile ground. After a period of private instruction with the bishop, Augustine and Alipius—along with Augustine's illegitimate son Adeodatus—were baptized by St. Ambrose on the night of the Easter Vigil, 387.

When Alipius renounced the Manichean heresy for

the Catholic faith, he also gave up the amphitheater. Strengthened by the grace of the sacraments, he never went to the gladiatorial games again.

Baptism seems to have drawn Alipius and Augustine even closer, with careers that followed identical paths. They both entered the priesthood and returned home to North Africa, where Augustine was named bishop of Hippo and Alipius bishop of their hometown, Thagaste. For the rest of their lives they were close collaborators, defending the faith against the Manicheans, as well as the Donatist and Pelagian heresies. The two friends died within a few months of each other: Augustine in 430, and Alipius in or around 429.

St. Patrick, Worshipper of False Gods

[*c. 390–c. 461*]   FEAST DAY: *March 17*

It didn't occur to the Catholic bishops of fourth-century Europe to send missionaries to such far-off lands as Ireland or Scandinavia. With so much of Europe still firmly heathen, there was more than enough work for missionaries close to home.

Ireland was off the radar in more ways than one. First, viewed from the cozy perspective of the Mediterranean, Ireland stood at the edge of the known world. Second, it was a country that had never been a province of the Roman Empire, and very little was known about the people and their customs. Third, it was an entirely pagan country, so missionaries would be immersed in hostile territory from the moment they set foot on Irish soil.

Of course, Providence does not conform itself to the agendas of bishops. Ireland became a bulwark of the Church thanks to one man who first entered the country as a slave, then returned as an apostle. It is interesting to note that this was not the first time a slave had introduced Christianity to a remote land. Christianity came to Ethiopia with St. Frumentius, a onetime slave to the king of Ethiopia, while St. Nino, a slave woman, was the mother of the Church in what is today the Republic of Georgia.

St. Patrick was born in a Roman settlement called Bannaventa on the British side of the Irish Sea. His mother, Concessa, and his father, Calpornius, were devout Christians who brought him up in the faith and taught their son the scriptures (Calpornius was a deacon). In spite of his parents' best efforts, Christianity made no discernible impact on Patrick. Late in life when he wrote his autobiography, the *Confession*, he admitted candidly, "I did not believe in the living God."

Patrick went on to acknowledge that when he was fifteen he did something so wicked that years later, when he was about to be ordained a deacon, he worried that perhaps his sin barred him from ordination. He disclosed the secret to his closest friend, who reassured him there was no impediment to receiving holy orders, and promised most solemnly never to repeat what Patrick had told him.

What had Patrick done? That question has tantalized historians and hagiographers for 1,600 years. Patrick himself doesn't give us much of a hint. He says it was something he "had done in my boyhood one day, nay, in one hour, because I was not yet strong." The traditional interpretation has been that Patrick had some kind of sexual encounter. Certainly, that is a possibility. But it is the reaction of Patrick's fellow bishops when his old friend went public with Patrick's secret that leads one to believe the sin was much more than some adolescent roll in the hay. Patrick says the bishops "attacked" him, that they started proceedings against him to strip him of the rank of bishop. "Not slight," Patrick says, "was the shame and blame that fell upon me."

Recently students of St. Patrick have suggested that the great sin of his youth was serious indeed. The current consensus is that Patrick, although technically a Christian, took part in a pagan ceremony. Such an offense truly would be bad enough that an old friend might feel obliged to reveal it, and members of the hierarchy might call for Patrick's removal from office.

The apostles had forbidden the first Christians to have anything to do with pagan rites; their prohibition even extended to eating part of any food that had been offered as a sacrifice to false gods. Where Patrick lived in Britain the old pagan rites were ubiquitous, while

Christianity was the strange, new religion. In the eyes of the Church, joining a dance around an oak tree or attending a sacrifice to a British god would count as participation in idolatry.

How then did an unbelieving, quasi-pagan youth become the great Apostle of Ireland and one of the Church's most renowned saints? When Patrick was sixteen a band of Irish raiders landed on the western coast of Britain near Bannaventa. They looted Calpornius and Concessa's villa and took Patrick himself captive.

In Ireland Patrick was sold into slavery and put to work watching sheep. Forced to live outdoors, exposed to heat and rain and cold, underclothed, underfed, far from home and with no hope of ever escaping from an island he described as "the utmost part of the earth," the boy was on the point of despair. Yet in that dark time Patrick at last remembered God. "The Lord opened the sense of my unbelief," he recalled, "that I might at last remember my sins and be converted with all my heart to the Lord my God." Perhaps for the first time since he was a child, Patrick began to pray, and with such fervor that as long as he was in conversation with God he was oblivious to frost and snow and rain. He says that he found the consolations of prayer so sweet he would offer one hundred prayers during the day, and another hundred during the night.

After six years in slavery, Patrick heard a voice say, "See, your ship is ready." At once, Patrick left the sheep and ran off to find the ship that would carry him home. When he arrived at the coast there was a ship preparing to leave, but the captain refused to take him aboard. As Patrick walked away, he prayed. He had not even finished the prayer before one of the crew called him back. "We will take you on," he said. "Make friends with us."

After a long, roundabout journey Patrick made his way back to his family in Bannaventa. Nor did he remain at home long. One night he had a dream in which a man gave him a letter that bore the inscription "The Voice of the Irish." When he opened it he heard a multitude crying, "We beg you, holy youth, come and walk among us once more." Certain of his vocation, Patrick left his home for Gaul to study for the priesthood in preparation for his return to Ireland as a missionary.

By the time Patrick was ordained there were a few Christians in Ireland, probably near present-day Wicklow. The size of this enclave was small, but sufficient to prompt the pope to send them a bishop named Palladius. He visited the Christians of Ireland, then sailed off to see the Christians of southwest Scotland. Before he could return to the Christian Irish, before a single mission had been sent to the pagan Irish, Palladius died.

In the 430s, or perhaps as late as the 450s, Patrick was ready to bring the faith to Ireland. He sold his patrimony to fund his mission and sailed across the Irish Sea, most likely coming ashore in Ulster (in his *Confession*, Patrick is maddeningly imprecise about places). He traveled extensively in Ulster, Leinster, and Munster; he may have gotten to Connaught on the west coast of Ireland, but that is uncertain. Yet everywhere he went he was astonished by the fervor with which the Irish responded to the gospel. In imagery that recalls St. Peter the fisherman, Patrick said, "[we] spread our nets so a great multitude and throng might be caught for God." Even more marvelous to him were the numbers of young men and women, many from the leading families of the country, who not only asked for baptism but begged to be permitted to take vows as monks and nuns.

If anything reveals the depth of Patrick's attachment to his converts it is the blistering letter he wrote to Coroticus, a Christian British prince who raided a Christian Irish community, killing many and carrying off the survivors to sell as slaves. Patrick denounced Coroticus and his men as "fellow citizens of the demons. . . . Dripping with blood, [you] welter in the blood of innocent Christians whom I have begotten into number for God and confirmed in Christ." In another passage it is obvious that the memories of his own years as a slave are still raw in Patrick's mind. "You . . . sell [Christians] to a foreign nation that has no knowledge of God. You betray the members of Christ as it were into a brothel."

There is no record that Coroticus ever released his captives, or that Patrick ever saw those beloved converts again.

We know that Patrick died on March 17, but we are not certain of the year: based on the surviving records, 461 is the best guess. He died justly proud of how far he managed to carry the faith among the Irish. In the centuries since Patrick's day, the Irish have carried that faith to every corner of the globe—to the United States and Canada, certainly, but also to Australia, New Zealand, Africa, and Asia, even back to England and Scotland. And wherever there are communities of Irish, invariably they build a church and name it after St. Patrick.

St. Mary of Egypt, Seductress

[c. 344–c. 421]   FEAST DAY: *April 2*

In the early years of the fifth century a priest named Zosimas lived in a monastery in the desert region near the Jordan River. The monks were renowned for their austere life, and they had adopted an unusual custom to prepare for Easter. Every year at the beginning of Lent they left their monastery, scattering throughout the desert to live as hermits. The community would not re-unite until Palm Sunday, when all the monks came home to observe Holy Week together.

One year, early in Lent, Father Zosimas was walk-ing in the desert when he saw someone near a low hill.

He was too far away to tell if it was a man or woman, but he could see that this individual was naked, with skin darkened by the sun and hair that was bleached white. As he approached, the stranger cried out, "Do not look at me! I am a woman, and naked as you see. Throw me your cloak so I can cover myself."

Father Zosimas turned his head, removed his cloak, and tossed it behind his back in the woman's direction. Once the woman was covered, she and the priest began a long conversation. Their talk is recorded in a sixth-century text entitled *The Life of Our Holy Mother, St. Mary of Egypt*. The little book is attributed to St. Sophronius (died c. 639), the patriarch of Jerusalem, but this is almost certainly a false attribution. It was common for scribes and copyists in the early centuries of the Church to attribute a document to a famous saint or bishop—it made the work more impressive, more authoritative. In all probability the life of St. Mary of Egypt was written about the year 500 by the monks of Father Zosimas's monastery. The book is not a meticulous biography but a record of an oral tradition, with a few unlikely supernatural embellishments thrown in for audience appeal.

To return to the encounter between Zosimas and the strange woman, she said her name was Mary, and she had been born in Egypt. When she was only twelve years old she ran away from home to live in Alexandria.

At this time Rome itself could not compare to the magnificence and wealth of Alexandria. All the trade goods of the known world flowed into its harbor and markets. Scholars and students came from Africa, Asia, and Europe to study in Alexandria's schools and world-famous library. But Mary was interested in something else: sexual adventures. She gave up her virginity soon after she arrived, and began a seventeen-year-long career of unbridled promiscuity.

Contrary to what some capsule biographies of St. Mary of Egypt say, she never became a prostitute. As she told Father Zosimas, "It was not for the sake of gain [that she invited so many men into her bed]. When they wished to pay me, I refused the money." She was not interested in wealth; she was interested in conquests. Eagerly she did "free of charge what gave me pleasure." She especially enjoyed seducing young men and instructing them in the arts of love. As she confessed to Father Zosimas, "There is no mentionable or unmentionable depravity of which I was not their teacher."

Mary came to regard herself as a skilled seductress, capable of getting any man she wanted. One day she saw a crowd of men waiting to board a ship in the harbor. A bystander told her the men were pilgrims about to sail for the Holy Land, where they planned to celebrate the Feast of the Exaltation of the Holy Cross in Jerusalem. The notion of seducing an entire passenger list appealed to Mary, so she joined the party. By the time the ship docked in the Holy Land, Mary had slept with every pilgrim.

The ship arrived in Jerusalem a few days ahead of the feast, so Mary occupied herself hunting men. On the feast day Mary joined the crowd heading to the Church of the Holy Sepulcher. She had no religious motive for going to church—she was simply curious to see the relic of the True Cross. As the throng entered the church, Mary felt an invisible force keeping her out. It made her angry to be excluded. She tried to approach the door from different directions, but still something kept her from crossing the threshold.

Now it began to occur to Mary that the powers of Heaven themselves were keeping her away from the Holy Sepulcher. Suddenly, the full realization of every-thing she had done broke upon her. Stranded outside the church, filled with shame and self-loathing, she wept and lamented as if her heart were breaking. Through her tears she saw an icon of the Blessed Virgin Mary above the entrance of the church. "Help me," she prayed to the Mother of God, "for I have no other help." Then Mary made a vow to give up her sinful life and to do penance.

Her prayer was answered. The force that had barred her way released her. Inside the church she at-tended Mass and venerated the relic of the Holy Cross.

As Mary exited the church she heard a voice say, "If you cross the Jordan, you will find glorious rest."

On the day she met Father Zosimas, Mary had been a hermit in the desert for forty-seven years. The first seventeen, she said, were the worst. She craved the rich foods she had enjoyed in Alexandria. She had loved the taste of wine, yet in the desert it was often difficult just to find water. Some days she could not get the lascivious songs she had once sung out of her head. And she felt strong sexual desires. In her temptations she called on the Blessed Virgin for help, and help always came. "After the violent storm," Mary said, "lasting calm descended."

Over the years her clothes turned to rags until they fell off her body. But since she never met anyone in the desert her nakedness did not trouble her.

When Mary finished her story, Father Zosimas bowed low to her, because he knew he was in the presence of a saint.

Then Mary asked the priest to do something for her. During the forty-seven years she had lived alone in the desert she had been deprived of Holy Communion. Next year on Holy Thursday, would Father Zosimas return and bring her Communion? The old monk promised.

The following year on Holy Thursday Father Zosimas took the Eucharist, and also a little food for Mary, and walked into the desert. On the banks of the Jordan Father Zosimas found Mary waiting for him and there he gave her Communion.

The next year the priest went to the Jordan again on Holy Thursday. He found Mary near the riverbank, but she was dead. The account of her life says that Zosimas tried to use a stick to dig a grave for the saint, but he was old and weak, and the ground was too hard. As the old monk wondered what to do, a lion came out of the desert. With its claws it dug a grave for Mary. After Father Zosimas buried the saint and said the prayers for the dead, the lion went back into the desert, and Father Zosimas returned home to his monastery to tell his abbot and his brother monks the story of Mary of Egypt.

St. Columba, Warmonger

[c. 521–597]   FEAST DAY: *June 9*

A traveler is hard put to find any monuments of early Christian Ireland. The passage of centuries, wave after wave of war and rebellion during England's occupation of the island, and the English Protestant dismantling of the Catholic Church in Ireland have all combined to reduce even the most important sites to piles of old rubble. St. Columba may have been born a prince of the O'Donnells, but there is nothing in County Donegal to suggest the power that clan once exerted there. The Rock of Doon, where the O'Donnell kings were installed, is just one more stone pinnacle in a landscape full of such craggy landmarks. As for Columba's birth-place, a Celtic high cross, erected in modern times, marks the site in an otherwise empty field. At the foot of the cross lies a slab of rock: legend says the saint's mother gave birth on this stone.

Although physical traces of Columba are scanty, his fame has never faded away, particularly among the Irish and the Scots, who revere him as one of their great-est national saints.

Like so many of his countrymen, Columba was mad for poetry and books. He was a newly ordained priest visiting St. Finnian at his monastery at Clonnard when he saw a beautiful Psalter Finnian himself had just brought back from Rome. It was an edition of St. Jerome's translation of the Psalms, rendered in flawless Latin. The book enchanted Columba. Night after night, after the monks had gone to sleep, Columba sat up copying the Psalter.

When Finnian discovered that Columba had been making a copy of his exquisite book, he demanded that Columba hand it over. Affronted, Columba refused. The quarrel grew so acrimonious that the two monks appealed to Diarmaid, Ireland's high king, to settle the question. Like a Celtic Solomon Diarmaid ruled, "To every cow its calf, to every book its copy." Columba was forced to surrender the copy he had toiled over through many long nights.

But this ancient case of copyright infringement did

not end there. Columba returned home to his monastery, angry and humiliated, trying to suppress his desire for revenge.

Not long after Diarmaid had ruled against Columba, a man from Connaught named Curran entered a hurling match. By accident he killed one of his opponents, a man related to Diarmaid. In fear for his own life, Curran fled to Columba's monastery for sanctuary. Columba sheltered the frightened man willingly and was just beginning the process that would clear Curran of a charge of homicide when the king's men-at-arms arrived at the door. The monks tried to bar the soldiers' way, but with weapons drawn the warriors scattered the holy men, then rushed right up to the altar where Columba held Curran in his arms, trying to shield the refugee with his own body. In the intense struggle that followed, Diarmaid's men threw Columba aside, dragged Curran out of the church, and killed him.

Enraged by this second insult at Diarmaid's hands, Columba appealed to his clansmen to avenge the family's honor, not to mention the rights of God, since the law of sanctuary had been violated. The O'Donnells rallied around their kinsman, declaring war on the king. At a place called Cooladrummon, beneath the County Sligo landmark known as Ben Bulben (made famous in the William Butler Yeats poem), the two armies met. Columba stood behind his clan, his armies stretched in the form of a cross, praying to God for victory. Diarmaid had brought along Finnian, who assumed the same position behind the king's troops. In the ferocious battle that followed three thousand men were slaughtered. The O'Donnells won the day; Columba felt vindicated.

The bishops and abbots of Ireland did not see it that way. At Telltown in Meath the leading churchmen of the country met to discuss the disgraceful incident. As the instigator of the battle, Columba was liable for excommunication. Only an appeal from his friend St. Brendan of Clonfert saved him from being excluded from the Church. Instead the synod voted for exile, ordering Columba to atone for his crime by bringing as many converts into the Church as died at Cooladrummon.

Columba's first biographer, Adomnan, makes no mention of the dispute over the Psalter or the violation of the right of sanctuary. While he does mention the synod of Telltown's threat to excommunicate Columba, Adomnan doesn't say what Columba did to deserve such censure. To set his readers' minds at rest, Adomnan assures us that the bishops and abbots were overreacting, that Columba's fault was "trivial and very pardonable." Then, for good measure, Adomnan says that besides, the process of excommunication discussed at Telltown would not have conformed to accepted ecclesiastical standards of due process.

If Adomnan sounds defensive, he was. Columba was a member of Adomnan's family, and although they had never met (Columba died almost thirty years before

Adomnan was born), kinship in Ireland could be, as we have seen, a very potent thing.

Obedient to the synod, Columba prepared to leave his homeland. Twelve monks, all blood relations, volunteered to go with him. It is likely that they sailed from the harbor of Derry, where Columba had founded a monastery. They steered their little boat north until they landed on the Scottish island of Iona, off the coast of the larger Isle of Mull. It wasn't much of a place—flat, rocky, its soil too poor for farming—but to the early Irish monks enduring the rigors of exile in a harsh landscape was not only a praiseworthy act of penance, it was heroic. The monks called such exile "the White Martyrdom," to distinguish it from the more commonly understood form, "the Red Martyrdom," in which the Christian sheds his blood for Christ. Among the Irish at this time, to leave Ireland, to sever ties with one's family, was a sacrifice so hard to make that God would most certainly take notice and shower the exile with blessings. Columba found his banishment so painful that he set up his cell on the side of the island where he could not see the coast of Ireland on the horizon.

As Columba and his monks began to build a monastery for themselves on Iona, a message came from Conall, the king of the Scottish province of Dalraida. He was deeding title of the island to Columba and his monks forever. (By the way, King Conall was also related to Columba.)

Some of the Scots in Dalraida were Christian, so for the first two years Columba and his companions focused their attention on building up the Church on the western edge of Scotland. Meanwhile, Columba prepared for a mission to the Picts, the ancient inhabitants of Scotland, who were still pagan, still following their druids in the worship of a host of gods and spirits of the natural world.

Before he began this mission Columba sent to Ireland for help. Two distinguished monks joined him in Iona, St. Canice (or Kenneth) and St. Comgall. They decided to start by visiting the Pictish king, Brude of Inverness. The king, however, refused to see the missionaries and had the gates of his stronghold barred against them. But when Columba raised his right hand and made the sign of the cross, an unseen hand pulled back the bolts and pushed the massive gates open.

Impressed by the miracle, Brude gave the three Irishmen permission to preach in his kingdom. In later centuries Scotland's kings would claim that Columba converted all the Picts. That is probably an exaggeration. Adomnan tells us Columba crossed Scotland, from east to west, two or three times, and that he preached the gospel in Skye, Kintyre, and along Loch Ness, where Columba had an interesting encounter.

He found a funeral in progress. The mourners said the dead man had been swimming in the loch when a sea monster attacked and killed him. As the mourners told their story, Columba observed another man swimming in the loch. As if on cue, the monster rose out of the water and lunged at the foolish swimmer. Columba made the sign of the cross, then commanded the beast to leave the man unharmed and return to the depths of the loch. To the amazement of everyone onshore, the monster obeyed.

Adomnan's story is the first written account of a monster in Loch Ness.

In his later years Columba was too infirm to go on missionary journeys. He settled into a quiet life at Iona, a gentle, genial abbot who spent his days writing poetry and copying books for libraries. He was transcribing the Psalms when he reached the verse "They that seek the Lord shall not be deprived of any good thing" (Psalm 33:11). Setting down his pen he said, "Here I must stop; let Baithin do the rest." Baithin was the monk Columba had named his successor. And, of course, Baithin was one of Columba's cousins.

That night as the monks filed into the dark church for matins they discovered Columba collapsed before the altar. He could not speak, but he tried to bless his monks. With that final gesture, the old man died. "The whole church," Adomnan says, "resounded with loud lamentations of grief."

St. Olga, Mass Murderer

[*c. 879–969*]   FEAST DAY: *July 11*

The founders of Russia's first royal family were not
Slavs, but Vikings. Rurik (c. 830–79), the first prince of
Novgorod, in what is now Ukraine, was just one in a
steady stream of Scandinavian warrior-adventurer-
traders who sailed down the Volga and the Dnieper
rivers in search of plunder or, when in a less aggressive
mood, in search of a good deal on furs and slaves.

In Rurik's day tribes populated the immense land-
mass that we call Russia. There was no czar, no central
political authority, and not many towns—Novgorod being one of the exceptions. Reliable historical accounts

from this period are hard to come by, so no one is certain how Rurik became prince of Novgorod. One version says that the people of Novgorod hired an army of Viking mercenaries led by Rurik to drive off an enemy tribe, the Pechenegs. The Pechenegs were fearsome warriors, but the Vikings were better. They scattered the Pechenegs, then returned to Novgorod, where they expected a hero's welcome. Instead, the Novgorodians and the Vikings quarreled—over what, no one can say. The quarrel escalated until the Vikings turned on the Novgorodians, conquered the city, and established Rurik as prince.

Rurik was succeeded by Oleg, in all probability his brother-in-law, who set about consolidating Viking power in the region, conquering neighboring tribes and establishing a new capital in Kiev. Oleg's reign marked the beginning of centralized power in Russia.

Olga entered this dynasty by her marriage to Oleg's son and heir, Igor. As prince of Kiev, Igor continued his father's policy of subduing more and more tribes and extracting tribute from those tribes that were too difficult to subjugate completely. The Drevlians were among the tribute payers. They had tried to shake off the prince of Kiev during Oleg's life, had rebelled at the time of Oleg's death, and in 945 had risen up again, refusing to pay their annual assessment to Igor.

With a large armed force Igor set out for Iskorosten, the Drevlians' chief town (today known as Korosten, on the Uzh River). Confronted with this show of force, coupled with threats of worse to follow, the Drevlians backed down and paid Igor what they owed him. It was a happy ending, yet as the prince and his army rode home to Kiev, Igor convinced himself that considering all the trouble the Drevlians had caused, they ought to cough up more. After ordering his men to carry the tribute home, Igor turned his horse around and headed back into the Drevlian territory, determined to coerce a supplemental payment from them.

Without his army, Prince Igor did not look nearly so dangerous. The Drevlians murdered him, then dumped his body in a hastily dug grave. Meanwhile the chief men of the tribe began to scheme: if Igor's widow Olga married Mal, their chief, the Drevlians would be princes and all the other tribes would fall under their rule. Igor and Olga's son, Svyatoslav, was not a consideration: he was a young boy whom they could bully now and dispose of later. Thoroughly pleased with their scheme, the Drevlians chose twenty of their most distinguished men to bring the news to Olga.

Olga must have been a shrewd customer. When the Drevlian embassy arrived at her door with news that Igor was dead, Olga gave them a gracious welcome. Encouraged by her cordiality, the ambassadors put aside diplomacy for perfect candor: they admitted their people had killed Igor, adding that since he was "like a wolf, crafty and ravening," he had it coming. But along with this sad news they had a proposal for Olga: their prince, Mal, was eager to become her husband.

Suppressing her grief and rage, Olga gave the Drevlian ambassadors a pleasant answer. "Your proposal is pleasing to me," she said. "Indeed my husband cannot rise again from the dead." Nevertheless, she did want to think it over. Olga suggested the ambassadors return the next day for her answer. After the Drevlians had gone their way, Olga commanded her servants to dig a deep ditch beside her stronghold.

The next day the ambassadors returned, dressed in all their finery, ready to hear Olga confess her willingness to become their princess. Instead Olga ordered her guard to seize the Drevlians and throw them into the pit. From the edge of the pit Olga called down to the envoys, inquiring how they liked their visit to Kiev so far. They cried, "Our case is worse than Igor's!"

And they were right. A quick thrust from a sword or spear had ended Igor's life, but the twenty ambassadors were about to be buried alive. As Olga turned away, she gave the order to fill in the pit.

Before the fate of the ambassadors could reach the Drevlians, Olga sent a message to Prince Mal: she had received his proposal of marriage, but if he wanted her to come to him, he must send the most distinguished men of his tribe to serve as her escort. From this message Mal imagined that his scheme to become prince of Kiev was progressing nicely. He sent the escort at once.

Once again Olga played the gracious hostess. She welcomed the Drevlians, even offering them the use of her bathhouse to clean up after their long ride. Once the last man was safely inside, Olga had her guards seal the doors and set fire to the building. Everyone in the bathhouse was burned alive.

Olga sent yet another message to Prince Mal. She was coming at last. But she wanted an opportunity to weep over her late husband's grave and honor his memory with a traditional funeral banquet. She asked Mal and all his most important men to be her guests and urged the prince to have plenty of mead on hand.

Outside Iskorosten Olga found Igor's humble grave. As her men heaped up a proper mound over their prince, Olga wept like a dutiful wife. With the funeral rites complete, Mal led Olga into his hall for the traditional feast. He asked about the escort he had sent to her. Olga replied that they were on their way, accompanied by Igor's personal bodyguard.

Acting as hosts, Olga and her entourage kept the mead flowing. Prince Mal and his people were so delighted by how easily everything was going their way, no one noticed that Olga and her people were not drinking. When at last all the guests were stupefied with drink, the men of Kiev drew their weapons and set about the grim business of killing everyone in the hall. Our main source for this story, *The Primary Chronicle*, claims that five thousand men were slain. That number is probably a medieval exaggeration. But it is likely that Olga's men cut down in cold blood several hundred Drevlians.

Yet Olga's rage still had not run its course. She returned to Kiev, collected an army, and marched on Iskorosten. By now the Drevlians were terrified of this woman. They sent her a message, offering to pay anything she demanded in ransom, but Olga did not want money. She ordered her soldiers to set fire to the city. As flames engulfed the wooden houses and walls, the inhabitants streamed out the gates, running into the open plain between their burning city and Olga's army. Many of them were slaughtered by Olga's troops. The ones who survived Olga sold into slavery.

With the destruction of Iskorosten, Olga's desire for vengeance was satisfied.

Nine years later, in 954, Olga traveled to Constantinople. The chronicles do not tell us why. It's possible she wanted to form an alliance with the emperor Constantine Porphyrogenitos. In Constantinople, the greatest, richest, most luxurious city in the Mediterranean world, Olga converted to Christianity. Once again we have no details about her decision. Given her conduct when she returned home, we know that Olga's conversion was sincere, which makes it even more frustrating that we do not have any clue who or what influenced her to give up her cruel, pagan ways.

When Olga asked the emperor to serve as her

godfather, he countered by asking Olga to become his wife. She put him off, suggesting that he ask her again after her baptism. It was a clever move. In Kiev she ruled as a princess in her own right over a vast territory. In Constantinople she would have the grand title of empress, but no power. After the baptism, when Constantine repeated his marriage proposal, Olga had an answer: she could not marry him; Church law forbade a goddaughter to marry her godfather.

And so, Christian but still a powerful and independent princess, Olga returned home.

Filled with zeal for her new faith Olga built churches in Kiev, Pskov, and elsewhere. She tried to bring her people into the Church, but most of them resisted all attempts to convert them. When she invited missionaries from Germany to come preach in her lands, they were murdered by the people of Rus (the land that incorporated most of Ukraine and part of modern Russia). Even within her own family she made no converts. When she died, it appeared that her attempt to make Rus a Christian nation had been a colossal failure.

Nonetheless, what began with Olga would be brought to fruition by her grandson, Vladimir. The Russians and Ukrainians venerate her as "the first from Rus to enter the kingdom of God," giving her the title "Equal to the Apostles," because she brought the Christian faith to their land.

St. Vladimir, Fratricide, Rapist, and Practitioner of Human Sacrifice

[c. 956–1015]   FEAST DAY: July 15

St. Olga died without ever seeing her countrymen adopt Christianity. Even her own family remained aggressively pagan. Her son, Svyatoslav, rejected Christianity as a feeble religion that would cost him the respect of his men. As Svyatoslav brought up his children in Rus's pagan religion, it seemed likely that Olga's death would mark the end of Christianity in Rus (the territory that covered most of Ukraine and part of Russia).

Svyatoslav may not have approved of his mother's religion, but he did appreciate her political alliances. Like Olga, he tried to keep on good terms with the emperor in Constantinople. A Byzantine chronicler named Leo the Deacon has left us a description of Svyatoslav at the time that he traveled to Constantinople to sign a treaty with Emperor John Tzimiskes. "He was of medium height," Leo writes, "broad-shouldered, with a long and luxurious moustache. His nose was stubby, eyes blue and eyebrows bushy, and his head was shaven apart from a lock on one side, which was a sign of nobility. In one ear was a gold ring with two pearls and a ruby between them. His white gown differed from his men's only by being cleaner. He appeared brooding and wild."

Like his father, Igor, Svyatoslav tried to expand Rus's power over the neighboring tribes. To gain leverage against the might of Byzantium, he allied himself with the Magyars and the Bulgars. When the Khazars, a tribe on the Volga River, resisted him, Svyatoslav destroyed them. Yet Syvatoslav's reign was brief: at age thirty-five he was killed while battling the Pechenegs. His enemies chopped off his head to make a drinking cup from Syvatoslav's skull.

As an illegitimate son, Vladimir did not succeed his father as prince of Kiev. The crown passed to Svyatoslav's eldest legitimate son, Yaropolk. But Vladimir refused to submit to this arrangement. He traveled to Scandinavia, recruited a Viking army, then returned to Rus and deposed his brother. With Vladimir's connivance, an assassin murdered Yaropolk. Then Vladimir went to a convent where his widowed sister-in-law had taken refuge, dragged her out, and made her part of his harem.

Vladimir's harem was one of the most impressive things about him: all the chroniclers mention it. In addition to his seven wives, Vladimir kept eight hundred concubines, divided into groups of a few hundred each and housed in the major towns of his realm. No matter where his travels took him, there would always be a good cross-section of women on hand to keep the prince amused.

Vladimir was a man with few scruples, if any. Yet on some level he felt that by raping his sister-in-law he might have gone too far. To soothe his conscience and placate the gods, he built an impressive temple in which he installed images of all the gods of Rus, along with the gods of the Turkic tribes—just to be on the safe side. To prove his seriousness to the gods he made the ultimate offering: human sacrifice. Vladimir chose the victims himself: Theodore, a proven warrior from his own band, and Theodore's young son, John, both of whom were Christians. Perhaps Vladimir believed the sacrifice of men who had turned their back on the old religion would appeal to the gods' sense of justice.

Like his grandfather and his father, Vladimir kept up his dynasty's program of conquest. With each new victory he replaced tribal chiefs with one of his own chosen men, sometimes even with one of his many sons.

Vladimir's power increased until he achieved the highest sign of respect any barbarian king could hope for: recognition from Christian monarchs. King Boleslav of Poland sealed a treaty with Vladimir. When Emperor Basil II faced the double threat of a revolt in Asia Minor and an invasion from the Bulgars, he turned to Vladimir for help. Out of respect for the treaty his father had made with Emperor John Tzimiskes, Vladimir led an army of six thousand men to assist Basil. In return, he wanted Basil's sister Anna as his wife.

It would be difficult to overestimate the outrage this request provoked among the nobility of Constantinople. No Byzantine princess had ever married a foreigner, let alone a heathen polygamist who indulged in human sacrifice and kept a small army of concubines. The dilemma put Basil in a difficult spot, but in the end he decided to dispense with precedents and promised his sister to Vladimir on the condition that Vladimir convert to Christianity and abandon his evil habits. To everyone's surprise, Vladimir agreed. True to his word he brought his army to Constantinople and helped Basil put down the rebels and drive back the Bulgars. Then, so the emperor would not forget their deal, Vladimir seized the wealthy Byzantine town of Kherson in the Crimea.

Basil took the hint and informed Anna that she would have to marry the prince of Kiev. Weeping bitterly, the twenty-five-year-old princess accused her brother of selling her like a slave. Considering how Vladimir regarded most of his women, Anna's analogy was no exaggeration.

Nonetheless, Anna was shipped off to Kherson, where the bishop of the town first baptized Vladimir, then married him to the princess. Vladimir showed his good faith by returning control of Kherson to Basil. With all parts of the bargain fulfilled, Vladimir escorted his new bride home to Kiev, where he surprised his in-laws and shocked his own people. Vladimir gave up his stable of wives and dissolved his harem. He laid out the advantages of Christianity to his entourage, urging them to set a good example for the people of Rus by converting. To keep in their prince's good graces, many of Vladimir's inner circle took the hint and asked to be baptized.

Everyone—Anna, Vladimir's retainers, his warriors, the ordinary people of Rus, the clergy who had come with the newlyweds to Kiev—believed Vladimir's conversion had been motivated by political considerations. They were wrong: Vladimir's conversion was genuine. He destroyed the images of the gods and the great temple he had built to house them. He invited architects from Constantinople to come build churches throughout Rus. He gave vast sums of money to assist the poor, tend to the sick, and relieve the homeless. He even abolished the death penalty. Impressed by the depth of their prince's change of heart, many people of Rus embraced the Christian faith. Grandmother Olga's prayers had been heard at last.

Vladimir died in 1015 and was buried in the Church of the Assumption of Our Lady, one of the first churches he had built in Kiev. Sadly, no trace of Vladimir's tomb or relics survived: his church and everything in it were destroyed in the wars that tore Russia apart during the twelfth and thirteenth centuries.

St. Olaf, Viking

[c. 995–1030]   FEAST DAY: July 29

"Viking" is both a noun and a verb. In the language scholars call Old Norse (which survives virtually unchanged today as the national language of Iceland), a *viking* is a raider, a freebooter, a pirate. To go *"viking"* means to sail off in search of plunder and adventure. In pre-Christian Scandinavian society, this was a perfectly acceptable, even heroic way of life that taught adolescent boys how to fight, how to sail, and, if luck went with them, to acquire enough loot to jump-start their fortunes back home.

Viking voyages brought wealth and slaves into the

northern lands, opened new markets for Scandinavian furs and other goods, even extended Scandinavian political influence into new territories. By the year AD 1000, descendants of the Vikings occupied the eastern half of England, dominated Irish society in Dublin (a city they had founded), and made up the ruling class in Normandy and in Kievan Rus, a vast region we know today as Ukraine.

There has been a tendency in books and movies to romanticize Vikings as robust, roistering, wild men. To the inhabitants of the coastal towns of Europe who were on the receiving end of the Viking raids, there was nothing romantic about them. On June 8, 793, the first Viking attack fell on Lindisfarne, today known as Holy Island, and famous in Britain for the shrine of St. Cuthbert, one of the country's best-loved saints. Those monks the Vikings did not slaughter on land they dragged out to sea and drowned. What they could not carry off, or what had no value to them—books especially—they destroyed. But the gold, silver, and ivory sacred vessels, reliquaries, and church ornaments they took with them. From this initial raid the Vikings learned that monasteries were rich and easy pickings; they targeted them on all future raids. Between 795 and 842, no fewer than twenty-six monasteries in Ireland alone were pillaged and destroyed by the Vikings. Among the casualties were the island's principal religious centers, Armagh, Kildare, Glendalough, and Clonmacnoise.

Soon fleets of Viking ships were going after bigger game. In 843 the Vikings attacked Nantes, slaughtering the bishop, most of the clergy, and countless numbers of inhabitants. In 844 they attacked Seville but were driven back. In 845, with one hundred ships, the Vikings sailed up the Seine and looted Paris. In 859 they sailed to Italy, where they plundered and destroyed Pisa. The years 865 to 895 saw an immense Viking army the Christians called "the Great Heathen Host" ravaging Britain, France, and Belgium.

Olaf was only twelve years old when his father entrusted him to an experienced raider named Hrani. On raids in the Baltic Sea Olaf learned to pillage, kill, and rape with a clear conscience. In the colorful metaphors of the Norse sagas, by his warlike exploits Olaf had "sated the wolf's brood," "roused the steel-storm," "convened the assembly of arrows."

The boy was about sixteen when he gave up the Viking life to serve as a mercenary against the English under a Norse chief named Thorkell the Tall. At London, Olaf constructed a booby trap near the Thames River that drowned dozens of English defenders. He led the vanguard at Canterbury, slaughtering civilians and burning the city's castle. Olaf's service under a Norse lord took him to Rouen, the primary city of the new Norse settlement known as Normandy. There Olaf converted to Christianity and was baptized in about the year 1013. Norse chronicler Snorri Sturlason, who knew Olaf and whose *Saga of Olaf Haraldson* is the most detailed biography we have of the man, does not explain Olaf's motives for becoming a Christian.

If Snorri doesn't tell us what was going on inside Olaf's head, he does at least give us an idea of what the man looked like. He was of middle height, but very strong; his hair was light brown, his skin pale with ruddy cheeks.

In 1015 Olaf returned home to Norway determined to make himself king and make his people Christians. He deposed King Hakon, then crushed his enemies in battle at Oslofjord. He made Nidaros (modern Trondheim) his capital, and there he built a church dedicated to the martyr-pope St. Clement. As king he enforced the law fairly, making peace and the security of his people his primary objectives. From that perspective, Olaf sounds like a conscientious Christian monarch. In many other respects, however, Olaf just didn't "get" the Christian ideal.

The king of Sweden claimed several districts in Norway as his own and sent twenty of his men into the countryside to collect taxes. Olaf displayed his contempt for Sweden's claim by having the foreign taxmen hanged and leaving their bodies on the gallows to rot.

Some Norse chieftains, jealous of Olaf's power, plotted to murder him. Unknown to the conspirators, one of the men they had invited to the meeting, Ketil, was loyal to Olaf. When Ketil revealed the details of the plot, Olaf received the news calmly. First he went to Mass. Then he went to dinner. Finally, with four hundred of his warriors, he sailed all night to a place called Ringsaker where the chiefs were staying. At daybreak the chiefs awoke to find themselves surrounded and outnumbered by Olaf's army. Olaf had the leading conspirator blinded, and another's tongue cut out. Two other chiefs he banished. As for the conspirators' retainers, he mutilated some, confiscated the estates of others, and exiled the rest.

Nor was the king a gentle proselytizer. There was a political dimension to Olaf's resolve to make Norway Christian. As the last pagan region of western Europe, Scandinavia was outside the cultural mainstream of the Continent. Christian kings were reluctant to enter into alliances with pagan Norsemen. And the ordinary Christian inhabitants of Europe regarded the Norse as blood-crazed, heathen barbarians. It was essential to Olaf's policy to place Norway on par with other Christian kingdoms, and he would not let anyone or anything stop him.

He brought in missionary priests from England, but at the head of the Church in Norway he placed a Norse bishop, Grimkell. The conversion of Norway proved to be a slow, tedious business, and Olaf was in a hurry to get the job done. With three hundred of his best men-at-arms he marched to those regions of Norway where resistance to Christianity was strongest. He destroyed pagan temples and smashed images of pagan gods. Anyone, of whatever rank, who would not abandon paganism risked execution, or blinding, or having a hand or foot lopped off. As Snorri tells us, the king "let none go unpunished who would not serve God."

It's interesting to note that Olaf's brutal, violent approach to converting a brutal, violent society worked. By 1030, Norway was a Christian country, nor did it backslide into paganism after Olaf's death.

Olaf's only political rival in Scandinavia was Knut, king of Denmark and of England. But with half the island of Britain recognizing the Anglo-Saxon contender, Aethelred, as their king, Knut had been occupied for many years in England, fighting to strengthen and expand his authority there. About the year 1026, when he had some breathing space, he turned his attention back to Scandinavia. Knut asserted that Norway was part of his kingdom, a claim Olaf rejected. Rather than attack Olaf outright, Knut was cunning. He flooded Norway with bribes, buying the allegiance of great lords and small landowners alike. In 1028, when Knut invaded Norway with a huge fleet, so few men rallied to Olaf's side that he was compelled to flee to Kiev, to the court of his kinsman Yaroslav (the son of St. Vladimir).

When Olaf went into exile he took with him his concubine, Alfhild, and their son, Magnus, whom he had named for Charlemagne (Karla-Magnus in Old Norse). His wife, Astrid, and their daughter, Ulfhild, Olaf left in Norway. Once again, in certain areas Olaf had not managed to reconcile within himself the demands of

Christian morality and the standards that were perfectly acceptable in pagan Norse society.

Olaf's banishment did not last long. In the summer of 1030 he sailed back to Norway at the head of an army. At a place called Stiklestad, Olaf drew up his forces to meet his enemies. Snorri says the day began in the classic saga style, with the king rising early and commanding a skald to recite a battle poem that would fire up the men. Once Olaf's warriors were arrayed for battle, he gave them their battle cry, "On! On, Christ's men! Cross-men! King's men!"

For hours the armies hacked and slashed at each other, with neither side gaining the upper hand. When a solar eclipse darkened the sky, each side feared the portent was for them. If it was an omen, it was for Olaf. He was fighting near a large boulder when three of Knut's warriors came at him at once. One crippled him, striking him above the knee with an axe. Another speared him in the belly. The third sliced open the left side of his neck. Gripping the stone with one hand, Olaf slipped slowly to the ground and died. At the death of the king, Olaf's men scattered.

After the battle, one of Olaf's retainers, Thorer Hund, returned to the field to claim his lord's body. He laid it out straight on the ground, covered it with a cloak, and wiped away the blood from the king's face. During the battle a sword had slashed Thorer's fingers, but when Olaf's blood touched the wounds they healed instantly. Later that same day a blind man inadvertently dipped his fingers in Olaf's blood. He ran his hand over his face and at once he could see.

In the eleventh century individual bishops had the authority to canonize people from their own diocese; now Bishop Grimkell exercised his right, declaring Olaf a saint. It was a canny move on Grimkell's part, one that gave the Norse Christians a native-born saint and a royal martyr, while at the same time placing Olaf's cause firmly on the side of right. Still, it was the type of canonization that could only have been carried out by the fiat of a local bishop who had in mind the needs of the local church rather than how his saint would play in the universal Church. It is safe to say that under the formal process of canonization that has been in place in the Catholic Church for the last several hundred years, Olaf would never have made the cut.

Grimkell enshrined the king's body in the Church of St. Clement in Nidaros, where it remained until 1070, when a handsome cathedral was built in honor of Norway's first saint. For the next five hundred years his tomb was a goal of pilgrims from throughout Scandinavia and northern Europe. When Scandinavia became Lutheran in the sixteenth century, the pilgrimage to St. Olaf's shrine came to an abrupt end. According to the Reverend Knut Andresen of the Nidaros Cathedral, in 1584 the cathedral clergy hid the relics of St. Olaf somewhere inside the church. They have never been found.

St. Thomas Becket, Hedonist

[c. 1120–1170]   FEAST DAY: *December 29*

His name was Thomas Becket. Not Thomas à Becket—
which he never used and no one ever called him until
sometime after the Reformation, when the odd name began to crop up in books, perhaps because it had a more
medieval ring to it, or perhaps because people were confusing their Thomases: there was Thomas Aquinas, the
great theologian, and Thomas à Kempis, the author of
Imitation of Christ. But the Thomas we will be discussing
was just plain Becket.

Nor was he a Saxon. The portrayal of Thomas as a
lowborn Saxon upstart bossing around Norman nobles

has no basis in history. It is a plot device from the 1964 movie *Becket*, starring Richard Burton and Peter O'Toole.

The real Thomas Becket was born in London on the afternoon of December 21, probably in the year 1120. By the liturgical calendar of the time it was the feast of St. Thomas the Apostle, so the infant's parents, Matilda and Gilbert, gave their son the name "Thomas" at his baptism.

The family came from Norman merchant stock. Gilbert emigrated from France to England as a young man. In fact, he and Theobald, archbishop of Canterbury, both hailed from the same part of Normandy, near the town of Thierville. We know that once, at some function or other, the merchant and the archbishop enjoyed a pleasant conversation together, swapping news about neighbors and relatives back home in the Old Country.

We know almost nothing about Matilda, except that she was keen on education for her boy. From age ten until he was twenty-one, Thomas studied first at the Augustinian priory at Merton, fifteen miles outside London, then at a London school, and finally at the university in Paris. Thomas's clerk, John of Salisbury, recalled that his master had an excellent memory and a subtle mind that could find a solution to almost any problem. And Thomas was very handsome—all the chroniclers of his time mention his good looks. No one says, however, that Thomas Becket was affectionate, or friendly, or pleasant to be around. Archbishop Theobald, who purposely put Thomas on the path to a great career by making him part of his household, and King Henry II, who unintentionally set Thomas on the path to sainthood by compelling him to accept the office of archbishop of Canterbury, both loved the man. Thomas's feelings for the elderly archbishop and the young king were a mixed bag of respect, gratitude, and resentment.

Thomas, like all clerks in this period, was considered a member of the lower ranks of the clergy. The word "clerk" is derived from "cleric." They accepted the tonsure, in which the hair on the crown of the head was cropped in the style of a priest, and they took minor orders, the first formal steps toward ordination to the priesthood. These formalities did not compel any student to take final vows as a priest. They did not oblige him to remain celibate, nor bar him from any secular occupation later in life. Rather than imposing duties upon the man, becoming a cleric actually conferred privileges. A cleric who got into trouble was immune from civil law; his case was heard in an ecclesiastical court where penalties were much lighter. For example, a layman who stole something could expect to be whipped at the very least, and might be hanged. A cleric guilty of the same crime would be confined in a comfortable monastery and fed on bread and water for a few weeks. This dual system of justice would be the source for many of Thomas's later troubles.

Fresh from the university at Paris, Thomas landed

his first job as a clerk for a London banker named Osbert Huitdeniers ("Eightpence"). We don't know what salary Osbert paid his clerk, but it must have been enough to give Thomas a taste of the good life. He started overdressing; he took up hunting and falconry; he ran with a boisterous, frivolous, fashionable crowd of young men. But this was only the beginning. In 1146, at age twenty-six, Thomas traded up, leaving Osbert's bank to take a position as clerk to Theobald, archbishop of Canterbury, the most important, most powerful prelate in England. Very quickly the archbishop learned that his new clerk was exceptionally clever, a fine administrator, and skilled at settling disputes. Theobald trusted Thomas with diplomatic missions, sent him to the university at Bologna in Italy to study Roman and canon law, and ordained him a deacon so he could award the young man the archdeaconry of Canterbury, a plum assignment that brought with it an annual income of one hundred pounds. As a deacon Thomas was only one step away from the priesthood. Now he was obligated to remain chaste and forbidden to bear arms, gamble, or pursue any other activity that would disgrace his office and reflect badly upon the Church.

A running joke at the time, put in the form of a theological point for debate, asked, "Can an archdeacon be saved?"—the implication being that archdeacons lived so fast and so loose that their damnation was virtually a sure thing. As archdeacon of Canterbury Thomas did nothing to diminish the old prejudices against his office. He still went hunting, he gambled (shooting dice was his favorite game), his wardrobe became even more worldly and ostentatious, and his pride even more puffed up. To supplement his income he took money from serious sinners, letting them buy their way out of their penances. To all this Archbishop Theobald turned a blind eye, unwilling to admit there might be anything unsavory about his favorite protégé. Consequently, in 1155 when Thomas resigned from the archbishop's service to join the household of the new king, Henry II, old Theobald's heart was broken.

The young king made Thomas his chancellor, a post that brought him vast power and wealth. He began to live like a prince. A crowd of servants maintained his sumptuously furnished house. He indulged his taste for the hunt with new dogs, new horses, and new hawks and falcons, and acquired trained wolves that he took into the forests to hunt the wild members of their kind. He owned six ships, claiming they were necessary to transport him, his goods, his documents, and his household on missions back and forth across the English Channel. To his lavishly appointed table he invited knights, nobles, and high churchmen, as well as cardsharps, courtesans, and lechers.

When Henry went to war with France, Thomas joined him, not merely as a military advisor, but as a commander. The archdeacon of Canterbury buckled on chain mail and a helmet to lead his own band of hand-picked fighting men into battle. When the French king drove the English back at Toulouse, Thomas retaliated by attacking the small town of Quercy, burning it to the ground and slaughtering almost all the inhabitants.

One frigid winter day King Henry and Thomas were riding through London when they saw a poor old man shivering in the street. The king suggested that since Thomas was an archdeacon, it would be fitting if he gave his magnificent new fur-lined cloak to the poor man. Thomas refused. The king, in a merry mood, insisted, and tried to pull the cloak off his friend's back. The two fell to the ground, wrestling, until Thomas at last gave in and handed his cloak to the unfortunate man. It never occurred to the king or the archdeacon that making someone else's misery the excuse for a comic brawl was the height of callousness.

In 1161 Archbishop Theobald died. Theoretically the monks of Canterbury Cathedral and the bishops of the realm elected a new archbishop, with the king endorsing their candidate. In practice the king could, if he wished, name the archbishop himself. That is precisely what Henry intended to do. To Henry's way of thinking the Church in England had become too independent. After decades of existing under the royal thumb, churchmen now saw themselves as a distinct class in English society, loyal to the king but not subservient to him. They felt more closely bound to the pope, and as this link to Rome grew stronger, the king's ability to dictate policy to the English hierarchy grew weaker. Henry was determined to reassert royal authority over the Church, and an excellent way to begin was to name as archbishop of Canterbury a man of unshakable loyalty. That man was Thomas Becket. Henry pushed so hard for his candidate that the bishops and monks put aside their own judgment to give the king the man he wanted.

On June 2, 1162, Thomas the archdeacon was ordained a priest. On June 3 he was consecrated archbishop of Canterbury. In the days of feasting and celebration that followed, a band of jesters approached the new archbishop to request a reward for their performance. In the past Thomas had always treated players, musicians, and other wandering entertainers generously. Now he said, "I am not the man I was when chancellor. Church funds are for the Church and the poor. I have nothing to give you."

That statement marks the beginning of Thomas Becket's conversion from a worldly, ruthless king's man to a man of God and a defender of the rights of the Church. Not that the conversion was completed overnight. Thomas still had expensive tastes, and as the leading churchman in England he could afford to live very well. He still hunted, with his own personal pack of hounds. Furthermore, his pride was bruised by the size of his archdiocese: it was one of the smallest in England, much too small for a man who had once gallivanted about the realm on the king's business. To relieve his boredom, Thomas began making extended formal visits to other dioceses across England. When word of Archbishop Becket's high living and pointless journeys reached Pope Alexander III, he wrote to Thomas, offering him a little fatherly advice. "You must shut yourself in the church of Canterbury," Alexander said. "Reduce yourself to mere necessities, and do stop chasing about all over the country."

The monotony of church life ended in 1163, when Henry II made his first move to assert royal authority over the Church in England. He attacked the problem by way of the criminal clerics issue, arguing that Church courts treated clerical thieves, traitors, and murderers too leniently. The way the king saw it, if a member of the clergy was guilty of a serious crime, the Church court should strip the offender of his clerical status and hand him over to the state for a just punishment. Henry argued that he was not introducing any innovations to the English code of law, but returning to a venerable legal tradition. Thomas, speaking for the English bishops, replied that the clergy respected and recognized the laws of the state and would support them so long as they did not impinge upon the rights and liberty of the Church. As for criminal clerics, laymen did not possess the right or authority to sit in judgment on clergymen.

The squabble sounds petty to modern ears, but the fight was not about which court would pass sentence on some pilfering priest—that was just a smoke screen for the real conflict. Henry wanted to rule over the Church the way he ruled over his barons. Thomas knew this better than any man, but as archbishop he would not compromise the independence of the Church.

Over the next year the archbishop and the king both dug in, each becoming more extreme in their positions. Then the fight got personal. Henry charged Thomas with criminal mismanagement during his days as chancellor and imposed a fine of thirty thousand gold marks or one hundred eighty thousand pounds—an impossible sum Thomas could never pay. Worse, Henry's men were now accusing Thomas, to his face, of treason. In fear for his life, the archbishop of Canterbury boarded a rowboat with three supporters and headed for the coast of France.

The six years of Thomas's exile from England give even his most sympathetic biographers headaches. As a refugee he was even less open to finding some middle ground where the demands of the king and the rights of the Church could both be satisfied. After Thomas excommunicated his enemies in England, Henry rounded up all of Thomas's relatives—including infants—and drove them out of the country, in the teeth of bitter winter weather.

By 1170 even Thomas's two most steadfast supporters, King Louis of France and Pope Alexander, were exasperated with the archbishop. But Thomas had his reasons for holding firm. He knew Henry would not be content with a few concessions from an archbishop: he wanted complete control over the Church in his territory. As for the king, he had insisted upon Thomas for archbishop because he considered the man a friend and ally. What is more bitter than betrayal at the hands of a friend?

In 1170 mediators arranged for Henry and Thomas to meet. Seeing each other after so long a separation stirred up the old feelings of affection between the two men. Bit by bit over the next few months they and their representatives resolved the thorniest issues until, in December 1170, Thomas Becket could return home to England. As his ship sailed into Sandwich harbor, a huge crowd thronged the dock, eager to welcome their archbishop. His progress to Canterbury was one long holiday, with farmers and villagers lining the roads, cheering and chanting what the people of Jerusalem had called out when Christ entered the Holy City on Palm Sunday, "Blessed is he who comes in the name of the Lord!" Outside the cathedral precincts Thomas dismounted and pulled off his boots. As the cathedral choir sang the ancient hymn "Christ conquers! Christ reigns! Christ commands!" Thomas walked barefoot up the main aisle of his church to prostrate himself before the high altar.

If anyone in England believed that the archbishop had modified his views concerning the rights of the

Church, he was mistaken. In Thomas's absence, at Henry II's request, the archbishop of York, assisted by six other English bishops, had crowned young Prince Henry king of England. Crowning an English king was the exclusive prerogative of the archbishop of Canterbury. On Christmas Day, Thomas, with the authority of the pope backing him up, excommunicated the archbishop of York and the six other bishops who had made the mistake of assuming a privilege that belonged to the archbishops of Canterbury alone.

Henry was in Normandy, celebrating Christmas at a castle called Bur-le-Roi near Bayeux when word of the excommunications reached him. Exploding in one of his famous rages, he cried, "Will no one relieve me of this lowborn priest?" That's only an approximation of the king's actual words, since the sources all give different versions. The point is that Thomas's enemies believed they had a royal commission to kill the archbishop. Four knights, Reginald FitzUrse, William de Tracy, Hugh de Morville, and Richard le Breton, set out for Canterbury, their pockets jingling with coins for their traveling expenses, furnished by Roger of Pont l'Eveque, the excommunicated archbishop of York.

On the afternoon of December 29, 1170, the knights galloped into the cathedral precincts and demanded an interview with the archbishop. Thomas met them in his private quarters. The knights insisted that Thomas lift the excommunications. He refused, and the conversation degenerated from there, ending in mutual recrimina-tions, with the knights threatening the archbishop's life.

As the knights went outside to arm, Thomas's atten-dants tried to hurry him into the church, where the monks were singing vespers. Once Thomas was safely inside, several monks locked the church door. "A cathe-dral is not a castle," Thomas said, and reopened the doors himself. He was ascending the steps of the sanctu-ary toward the high altar when the four knights stormed into the church, their helmets and chain mail rattling, their swords drawn, shouting, "Where is Thomas Becket the traitor? Where is the archbishop?"

Thomas turned to answer. "Here I am," he said. "No traitor to the king, but a priest of God."

FitzUrse came up behind the archbishop, flicked off his skullcap with the point of his sword, grabbed the archbishop's cope, and tried to haul him outside. "Get out of here, you abominable man," Thomas com-manded. "I am not a traitor and don't deserve any such accusation."

FitzUrse gave a sharp tug on the cope, making Thomas stumble. The knight and the archbishop strug-gled until Thomas gave the man such a good shove that FitzUrse almost fell sprawling on the pavement. As FitzUrse regained his balance, Thomas let fly one final insult, "You pimp!"

Like mad dogs the knights closed in around the archbishop. "Now," one said, "you die."

A moment earlier Thomas had been brawling in his own cathedral; now he composed himself for martyrdom. Making the sign of the cross he said, "To God and to the Blessed Virgin Mary, to the blessed martyr Denis and to St. Alphege, archbishop of Canterbury, and to the patrons of this place I commend my spirit and the cause of the Church."

Crying, "Strike! Strike!" the knights hacked at the archbishop with their swords. Under a hail of blows, Thomas fell in the transept of the church, between the side chapels of Our Lady and St. Benedict. The four knights ran out a side door of the cathedral, but one of their attendants, Hugh of Horsea, went back into the church, placed his foot on Thomas's neck to steady himself, then thrust his sword into the fallen man's skull and scattered the brains across the floor. "Come on!" he cried to the knights. "He'll never get up again."

The murder of the archbishop in his own cathedral shocked England and all of Christian Europe. Martyrdom rehabilitated Thomas: he was no longer an obstinate prelate, but one of God's champions. Pilgrims who visited the murdered archbishop's tomb reported such a flood of miracles that barely two years after Thomas had been slain, Pope Alexander declared him a saint.

Henry, on the other hand, began to look like an outlaw. There was a real danger that rival monarchs might take Thomas's murder as an excuse to wage war on Henry. It was possible that Henry's own subjects would rebel against him. To restore his reputation Henry announced he would do public penance for the part he played in Thomas's death.

On July 12, 1174, the people of Canterbury watched as their king walked barefoot through a rainstorm to the cathedral. Down in the crypt, before the tomb of his old friend, Henry stripped to the waist. Each bishop present gave the king five blows across the back with a leather whip; the eighty monks of Canterbury gave the king three lashes each.

In spite of Thomas Becket's martyrdom and Henry II's penance, the balance between papal authority and royal power remained an unsettled issue in England until 1535, the year Henry VIII severed his nation's ties to Rome, declaring that he was the Supreme Head of the Church in England. Three years later he sent his agents to Canterbury. They stripped all the gold, silver, and jewels from St. Thomas's shrine and shipped them back to the royal treasury. Then they pried open the tomb and destroyed St. Thomas's remains. In Henry VIII's England there could be no challenge to the king, not even from a long-dead saint.

St. Francis of Assisi, Wastrel

[1182–1226]   FEAST DAY: October 4

It often happens that a hardworking, aggressive, entre-preneurial father builds the fortune, and his son squanders it. That's how it played out in the nineteenth century among the Vanderbilts, and it happened seven hundred years earlier in Assisi among the Bernadones.

Assisi in the twelfth century was in the same situation as many other Italian cities. There were the old aristocratic families like the Offreduccios (the family of St. Clare), who wanted to preserve the feudal system that kept them at the top of the social and political heap. Then there were the ambitious, up-and-coming middle class businesspeople like the Bernadones (St. Francis's family), who wanted Assisi to become a republic in which they would have a say in governing themselves. The split between these two factions was as much geographical as it was ideological: the nobles lived in their fortified palazzos on the hill near the Cathedral of San Rufino; the merchants lived in the lower end of town around the aptly named Piazza del Commune. That is where Francis was born, in a room above his parents' cloth shop.

Pietro di Bernadone and his wife Pica made a very good living as cloth merchants, and no doubt they expected their only child to follow in their footsteps. But a sober, respectable mercantile life did not appeal to young Francis. In a town filled with young unmarried men who had too much time on their hands, and too much money in their pockets, Francis tried to outdo everyone else in extravagant clothes, silly practical jokes, and all manner of foolery. With his friends he ran the streets all night, sometimes drinking in taverns, other times playing the part of an amateur troubadour singing outside a pretty girl's window. On a feast day, these boys were the life of the party. And when it came to squandering money, Francis would not permit anyone to surpass him.

His reputation for picking up the check attracted some of the worst young men in town. Before, Francis had been frivolous and thoughtless; with this new bad set,

Francis discovered the back alleys of Assisi, where, as he recalled later in his autobiography, *The Confessions*, "[I] wallowed in its filth as though basking in cinnamon and precious ointments."

Francis's notion that life was one long party took a dangerous turn when he was twenty years old. In 1202 the long-simmering feud between Assisi's aristocrats and middle class erupted into civil war. When the nearby town of Perugia threw its support behind the nobility, the non-noble population of Assisi drove the lords and ladies out of town. As the republicans of Assisi girded themselves for war, Francis enlisted. He had gotten the idea in his head that war was just one more bash in fancy dress. His misconception was cleared up in the one and only battle he ever fought, at Collestrada, where the men of Perugia scattered the men of Assisi, taking many prisoners—Francis among them. For the next year Francis and his fellow prisoners of war were confined to a dungeon. The filth, the rats, the bad food, the crowding, the smells, and the confinement all took their toll on Francis. He emerged from prison a profoundly depressed twenty-one-year-old man.

Back home he made an effort to return to the old life of drinking, dancing, and chasing pretty girls, but he had lost the joy of it. No one knew that during the day Francis would slip off to some quiet corner of a church, or to an unfrequented country chapel, and pray. In his depression this was the one activity that comforted him.

Nonetheless, there was a part of Francis that still wished he could be a thoughtless, pleasure-seeking boy again.

Francis was out riding one day when he had an experience that unnerved him. He saw a leper on the road. The old Francis had a deep-seated horror of leprosy and would have galloped away from the poor man. But to his own surprise, Francis found himself climbing down from his horse, kissing the leper's disfigured hand, and giving him a fistful of coins. Until now Francis thought the trauma of the dungeon had transformed him into a serious, committed, yet conventional Catholic. His reaction to the leper made him wonder if perhaps God was calling him to a more intense form of Christianity.

Outside the walls of Assisi stood the tumbledown chapel of San Damiano. Over the altar hung a painted wooden Byzantine-style crucifix that depicted Christ gazing directly at the congregation. In the fall of 1204, as Francis was praying before this crucifix in San Damiano, he saw Christ's lips move and heard a voice say, "Francis! Rebuild my church, which as you can see has fallen into ruins."

Taking the message from the cross literally, Francis hurried back to his father's shop. Pietro wasn't around. If he had been Francis would never have been able to pack up the finest cloth in the inventory and ride off to the city of Foligno to sell it. The cloth brought a good price, and Francis gave it all to the priest assigned to San Damiano.

As acts of charity go, this was exceedingly generous. But there was a snag that did not occur to Francis: the cloth was not his to sell. This point, however, did not escape Pietro. Enraged that both the cloth and the money were gone, he dragged his own son to court, demanding restitution. The judge in Assisi was the town's bishop, Guido. He ruled in Pietro's favor, ordering Francis to hand over the money. This was easy to accomplish since the stunned (and possibly suspicious) priest of San Damiano had not spent one penny. To all appearances the case was over, but conversion had not diminished Francis's taste for the flamboyant. Having given back the money, he decided to return everything else he had received from his father. Standing in the public square he stripped naked and handed all his clothes to Pietro. As the crowd buzzed with excitement at the spectacle, Bishop Guido hurried forward, unfastening his cloak as he came, and wrapped the mantle around Francis.

For the next three years Francis was a cause of shame to his parents and confusion to his friends. He wore a long rough robe and went about the streets of Assisi begging for food for himself and for alms to rebuild San Damiano. From the perspective of the down-to-earth Bernadones, if their son had a religious vocation he should enter a monastery, or train for the diocesan clergy. Panhandling was not piety, it was a disgrace. And to give the Bernadones their due, Francis did not have much of an idea of what God wanted from him.

On February 24, 1208, while attending Mass at the little church of St. Mary of the Angels (now known as the Portiuncula), Francis heard the priest read the gospel text in which Christ told his apostles they should "possess neither gold nor silver, nor money in your purses, nor scrip for your journey, nor two coats, nor shoes." This gospel was read out in the churches every year, so Francis must have heard it many times before, but on this day Christ's words pierced his heart. And once again, Francis took the words he heard literally.

Francis committed himself to a life of absolute poverty: he wore the bare minimum of clothing; he had no place to live; he had nothing to eat except what people gave him; he had no money; and he had no idea how he would provide for himself the next day. Christ had said his yoke was easy and his burden light, yet Francis clung to a vision of religious life so difficult to emulate that within his own lifetime his followers felt it necessary to soften their founder's principle of radical poverty.

Such qualms never touched Francis. His confidence that the Lord would provide was absolute. This trust in God's goodness spilled over into his preaching. Now when he spoke before crowds, he brought to his message of repentance and salvation the kind of exuberance and contagious joy he had once demonstrated when he stayed out all night singing troubadour songs. He caused a sensation in and around Assisi. Within a few weeks of Francis's revelation at Mass, half a dozen men had joined him as disciples. They called themselves the *frati minores*, the lesser brothers.

St. Francis's spirituality emphasized the humanity of Jesus—poor, abandoned, and crucified. The first Franciscans saw the suffering Jesus in the lepers, the destitute, the sick, and all sinners, and they began their mission among these forgotten, neglected people.

Just as he saw Christ in all men, Francis saw the splendor of God in all creation. The sight of lambs and flowers made him rejoice over the goodness of God, but he felt the same way when he saw spiders and worms. He celebrated the beauty of the universe in his renowned Canticle of the Sun. Some enthusiastic but misguided souls have mangled the meaning of the canticle, portraying Francis as a medieval pantheist or late-blooming pagan who worshipped sun and moon and wind and fire as gods. Good Catholic that he was, St. Francis would have recoiled at such a suggestion: he composed his canticle as a hymn the natural world sings to its Creator.

Whether he had intended to do so originally or not, Francis launched a new type of religious life within the Catholic Church. Previously the clergy fell into two categories: the monks, who lived apart from the world (with varying degrees of strictness, depending on the rule of the individual order), and the parish priests, who lived among the faithful. Francis's disciples formed a religious order that plunged into the thick of day-to-day life, where they performed works of charity and offered religious counsel to all comers. The Franciscan movement inspired men across Europe: by 1220 it had grown to five thousand members.

It has been said that St. Francis is the best loved of the saints because he most closely resembles Jesus Christ. In 1224 that likeness to his Lord took an exceptional turn. With a few companions Francis had gone into the mountains north of Arezzo for a forty-day religious retreat. On or around the Feast of the Exaltation of the Holy Cross, September 14, Francis had a vision. He saw a seraph, an angel with six wings, whose hands and feet were fixed to a cross. At the sight, Francis went into an ecstasy, and when he was himself again he found that his hands and feet and side were wounded with the marks of Christ's Passion. This is the first recorded instance of a phenomenon known as stigmata.

It is a natural impulse to revere the stigmata as a tremendous sign of God's favor. Francis, who had to live with it, found it troublesome. The stigmata made him self-conscious, especially as news of the miracle spread and curious people wanted to see the wounds. After years of going about barefoot, Francis started wearing socks and shoes to hide the wounds in his feet. To conceal his wounded hands he wrapped bandages around his palms and wore sleeves that fell past his fingertips. It was not simply a matter of masking the marks of Christ's Passion; the wounds were also painful. Once a brother Franciscan inadvertently brushed against Francis, chafing the wound in his side. Francis cried out in pain and slapped the man.

In September 1226 Francis fell ill. Too weak to write himself, he dictated a letter to a dear friend who lived in Rome, Lady Jacoba de Settesoli. Francis explained he was dying and begged her to come quickly to Assisi so they could see each other one last time. Then he asked her to bring along a shroud, candles, and incense for his funeral. And he wanted one more thing: a sweet almond confection that was Lady Jacoba's specialty.

Francis had just finished the letter when Lady Jacoba entered the room asking, "What is the news? Is Father Francis still alive?" In her house in Rome she had heard a voice tell her to hurry to Assisi, that Francis was dying. She had brought everything necessary for the Requiem Mass, and she had Father Francis's favorite pastry, too.

On the night of October 3 Francis of Assisi died. As the friars prepared the body Lady Jacoba urged them to uncover the stigmata so the mourners could see the miracle. Two years later, in one of the fastest canonizations on record, Pope Honorius III declared Francis of Assisi a saint.

Blessed Giles of Portugal, Satanist

[1185–1265]   FEAST DAY: May 14

During the Middle Ages it was the custom among well-to-do families with many children to designate one of their younger sons for the Church. As traditions go, this one was both pious and pragmatic. On the one hand, the parents were devoting one of their children to the service of God. On the other hand, they wouldn't have to worry how he would get along in the world with little or no inheritance. The custom did have one serious drawback: families rarely asked the designated son if he had a religious vocation. Such was the case with Giles of Portugal.

Giles's father, Rodrigues de Vagliatos, was governor

of Coimbra, Portugal's renowned university city. Upon the young man's ordination the king demonstrated his regard for Governor de Vagliatos by awarding him the benefices, or incomes, from a variety of parishes and religious installations. According to the corrupt system of the day, Giles received the money without ever setting foot in any of these parishes, let alone actually tending to the parishioners. (That job would be farmed out to some impoverished, lowborn priest.)

As a priest with an independent income and no religious obligations, Giles had plenty of time to engage in the field that did interest him: the study of the sciences. He began with medicine and physics, but soon he was conducting experiments in alchemy, the pseudoscience of the Middle Ages that consisted of equal parts magic and chemistry. Soon a rumor circulated through the university that Giles dabbled in black magic.

That last bit of academic gossip is probably the source for the most fantastic part of Giles's story. According to the legend, Giles's desire to know everything was so fierce that Satan himself appeared to make his classic offer: he would reveal to Giles all the secrets of the universe in exchange for Giles's immortal soul. Giles accepted the devil's offer, and even signed a contract to seal the deal.

For seven years Giles enjoyed honors, wealth, and the respect and envy of his fellow scientists. Then one night he had an awful dream. He saw Death carrying an hourglass as he walked through a graveyard. The specter stopped at a tomb where he called Giles's name, but the grave proved to be empty. Then Death lifted the hourglass and murmured, "Ah! Giles's sand has not yet run out."

Giles woke up screaming in terror. In the dark of night he threw a few possessions into a bag and ran. But where could a man hide from the devil?

Giles believed he had found a place to hide when on the road he met some Dominican friars. He begged to join their order, made his confession, and began a long period of penance. Nonetheless, he was still afraid that Satan would show up one day to carry his soul to hell. To shield himself from the devil, Giles turned to the Blessed Virgin Mary, begging her day after day to come to his assistance.

Giles had been a Dominican for seven years when one morning as he went to his place in the choir he found a scroll. Opening it he saw it was the pact he had signed with Satan. Mary herself had snatched it out of the devil's hands.

The insertion of the Dr. Faustus legend certainly livens up Blessed Giles's story, but it is not to be taken seriously. The historical Giles was a lax, corrupt priest who was converted by a chance encounter with some Dominicans. After joining their order he was assigned to the Dominican house in Santarem, Portugal, where his medical studies were put to good use in the infirmary. As penance Giles did all the dirty housekeeping work around the monastery, but it was to make amends for bringing disgrace on the priesthood, not for making a pact with Satan.

St. Margaret of Cortona, Rich Man's Mistress

[1247–1297]   *FEAST DAY: February 22*

In his biography of St. Margaret, Francois Mauriac, the French author and Nobel laureate, tells us that as a child Margaret possessed a sweet, loving temperament—as long as she got her way. She was so beautiful, so precocious, that her mother and father couldn't help spoiling her. But when Margaret was seven years old her happy little world collapsed. Her mother died, and very soon after her father remarried. Almost from the moment they met, Margaret and her stepmother hated each other.

The stepmother recognized Margaret for what she was: a pampered and willful child whom no adult had ever tried to curb. And so every day saw a battle of the wills between the girl and her stepmother. Margaret's father didn't help matters: one day he would side with his daughter, the next day he would side with his new wife. As she grew older, to escape the tension and quarrels at home, Margaret began to spend more and more time away from the house.

In the village the adolescent Margaret's good looks and quick wit attracted attention, especially the attention of older boys. Margaret, who would not let anyone tell her what to do, discovered that with a little skillful flirting she could get boys to do almost anything she wanted them to do. Whether Margaret had any sexual experiences with the village boys, we do not know. This much is certain, however: when Arsenio, the sixteen-year-old son of a baron, invited thirteen-year-old Margaret to live with him as his mistress, she accepted, apparently without thinking twice about it.

For Margaret her new life was idyllic. A rich young man said he loved her. He took her away to live in his castle. She had escaped the harsh life of a peasant and the scolding of her stepmother to live in ease and comfort, with servants who did everything for her. The only thing that marred Margaret's happiness was Arsenio's candid avowal that he would never marry her. Nonetheless, Margaret believed she could change his mind.

When she gave birth to Arsenio's son, she thought the baby would persuade him to marry her. It never happened. Poor Margaret never understood—or perhaps she could never bring herself to admit—that a nobleman might live with a peasant girl, but he would only marry a woman from his own social class.

Margaret had lived as Arsenio's mistress for nine years when he left the castle for a few days to tend to some business at one of his family's estates. He did not return on the day he was expected. Nor the day after. Nor the day after that. Now Margaret's anxiety level was rising, and she only felt worse when Arsenio's dog arrived back at the castle alone. The dog's behavior made Margaret nervous. It cowered in corners and whined. It walked in circles around Margaret, whimpering. Suddenly it took her skirt in its mouth and, backing up, pulled her toward the door. As Margaret followed the dog outside she felt a terrible sense of dread. The dog led her deep into the woods, then stopped at a pile of dead branches and dry brush where once again it began to whimper. Margaret's hands trembled as she cleared away the dead wood. Beneath the pile, lying in a shallow pit, she found Arsenio, dead and decaying.

Who killed Arsenio? No one knows. Perhaps bandits—the woods at the time were full of them. Perhaps the henchmen of a rival family—such vendettas were commonplace in Italy during the Middle Ages. But Margaret's mind was not on the culprits: for the first time in a long time she was thinking about the state of her soul. She and Arsenio had lived in sin together for nine years and had never been sorry about what they were doing. Now she wondered if at the last moment Arsenio had had time to repent. And she wondered, if death took her suddenly, would she have time, would she have the sense to beg God for his mercy and forgiveness?

Determined to make a fresh start, Margaret took her little boy, left Arsenio's castle, and headed for her father's house. Like the prodigal daughter that she was, she knelt at her father's feet and begged him to forgive her. The good man lifted up his daughter and with tears welcomed her home.

Margaret's stepmother did not offer any welcome, but she didn't start a family brawl, either. Her husband was delighted to have his daughter and grandson in the house, but the stepmother had a fair appreciation of Margaret's character: soon enough the penitent would do something new to alienate her father. Sad to say, the stepmother was right.

Entirely caught up as she was in her conversion, Margaret felt that it was not enough to go to confession and perform her penance. Since her sinfulness had been public, she felt that her repentance should be public, too. To start, she began to wear sacklike dresses made of rough material. On Sundays she put a noose around her neck and knelt outside the church door where all her neighbors could see her. Margaret's flamboyance irritated her father, but he wrote it off as a phase that would pass. Then one Sunday Margaret went too far.

Before Mass began, Margaret walked to the front of her village church, where she told the entire congregation all the sins she had committed during the nine years she had lived with Arsenio. That was too much for Margaret's father. He told her she had humiliated him before the entire town; she would have to leave.

Standing in the road outside her father's house Margaret faced two choices: she could continue her new life, or she could go back to her friends from her days as Arsenio's mistress. They would take her in, and in time she would probably drift back into the pleasure-seeking world she had known as a rich man's mistress. It was a tough decision for a young woman who liked to be pampered, but in the end Margaret turned her back on the castle and headed for the hilltop town of Cortona, where, she had heard, the Franciscan fathers helped repentant sinners.

The Franciscans of Cortona were kinder than Margaret had imagined. They found a home for her and her son with two sisters, Marinana and Raneria Moscari. They assigned two Franciscan priests, Father Giunta Bevegnati and Father John da Castiglione, to be her spiritual directors. When Margaret's son was old enough to go to school, the Franciscans arranged for him to live at a private academy in the nearby town of Arezzo.

If Fathers Bevegnati and da Castiglione thought Margaret was a run-of-the-mill bad girl, they were in for a surprise. The Moscari sisters reported that she slept on the floor, that she survived on a starvation diet, that she beat herself. What the Moscaris did not know was that Margaret was wrestling with powerful sexual temptations. She thought if she practiced strict discipline she could conquer her lascivious desires. The priests tried to get Margaret to modify her regimen of prayer and penance, but she argued back. "Do not ask me to come to terms with this body of mine," she said, "because I cannot afford it. Between me and my body there will be a struggle until death." In fact, she struggled against her sexual impulses until the end of her life.

Three years after her arrival in Cortona Margaret joined the Franciscan Third Order, which permitted her to take the vows of a nun and wear the habit of a nun, but live outside the convent. To make herself useful she founded a hospital for the poor in Cortona, then established two organizations, one for women, one for men. The women worked as nurses and administrators in the hospital. The men also assisted in the hospital, but their primary role was to get jobs to support it.

Spurred by Arsenio's sudden death, Margaret became especially devoted to the poor souls in Purgatory. For the rest of her life she prayed earnestly every day for the dead. When Margaret herself was dying, she had a vision of a vast company of souls streaming out of Heaven: they were the souls she had ransomed from Purgatory with her prayers.

Blessed Angela of Foligno, Gossip and Hedonist

[c. 1248–1309]   FEAST DAY: January 4

The thirteenth century was a watershed moment for western Europe. The expansion of international trade was transforming small shopkeepers into merchant princes, making some wealthier than the local barons whose income was still based on agriculture. In Italy especially, success made the merchants bold. In commercial centers such as Florence and Siena the rising middle class began to shake off their old feudal allegiances, taking the first steps toward becoming a republic on the model of ancient Rome.

Changes had come to religious life, too. New religious

orders, the Franciscans especially, offered a new ideal in which consecrated men and women did not retreat into a monastery or convent but carried their twofold mission of faith and good works into the streets.

Keeping pace with these shifts in church and society were the notions of what made a saint. Previously a local saint was likely to be a conscientious bishop or a dutiful abbot of a Benedictine monastery—men who occupied the upper echelon of religious life while also wielding authority over temporal matters. In the case of female saints, they also came from the upper ranks of society: queens, abbesses, or members of the most exalted noble families. A thirteenth-century saint, however, was more likely to come from the new middle class and the saint's reputation for holiness more likely to be based on personal humility and heroic acts of charity. It is interesting to note that in this down-to-earth era, mysticism became a popular sign of sanctity, particularly among women. The history of the thirteenth century is rich with stories of virgins, housewives, and widows who experienced intense visions, private revelations, and uninhibited ecstasies. In every respect, Blessed Angela of Foligno fit this new model of holiness perfectly.

We do not know anything about Angela's background, but we do know she was beautiful and she married a wealthy member of the town's middle class, who probably made his fortune during Foligno's commercial revolution. The cloth trade had made Foligno, a town about ten miles south of Assisi, an economic powerhouse; as the wife of a wealthy merchant Angela enjoyed every comfort and every luxury, and she wallowed in them. Her passions were expensive clothes and flashy jewels, extravagant meals and rare wines. She dressed and acted in ways that would provoke envy among women and sexual desire among men. Wealth and beauty made her proud; pride made her cruel. When she was not indulging herself, she spent hours gossiping with her friends and maligning her neighbors. If anyone crossed her or tried to correct her, she unleashed her vicious temper.

Angela tells us that in 1285 she did something so bad that for the first time she began to live in fear of Hell. Her biographers speculate that Angela committed adultery, and given the intensity of her guilt and shame that seems likely. She went to confession to unburden herself of her sin but in the confessional lost her nerve and purposely concealed her sin from the priest. In Catholic theology, it is a serious offense to make a bad confession, yet Angela compounded it by receiving Holy Communion afterward. . Now she could add sacrilege to her list of sins.

Near despair, she prayed to St. Francis of Assisi to direct her to a skilled confessor. As Angela prayed the saint appeared to her and said, "Sister, if you would have asked me sooner I would have complied with your request sooner. Nonetheless, your request is granted."

That same day Angela went to Foligno's Cathedral of San Feliciano to pray and found the confessor she was looking for. In the pulpit stood a Franciscan priest, Father Arnoldo, one of the bishop's chaplains and one of Angela's relatives. After his sermon, she asked Father Arnoldo to hear her confession, and this time Angela disclosed all her sins.

Angela left the cathedral that day resolved to begin a new life. She sold her fine clothes, her jewels, and her costly toiletries to relieve the poor and suffering of Foligno. It was a good start, but she was still a wealthy woman, with temptations to self-indulgence on every side. Later, as she dictated her autobiography to Father Arnoldo, she recalled that during the first five years of her conversion her spiritual life progressed "only small steps at a time."

It was a family tragedy that freed Angela. In a very short period her mother, her husband, and all her sons died. As a widow and heiress of a considerable estate she could do as she pleased, so Angela began to sell everything she owned.

Her spiritual directors warned that she was being excessively zealous. They had known other wealthy women who had given away all their property only to discover too late that they had no vocation for a life of poverty. Angela recognized this was sound advice. To give herself time to reflect on what she wanted to do, she made a pilgrimage to Rome. By the time she reached St.

Peter's she was convinced that she was intended for a life of prayer and sacrifice. Back home in Foligno she sold off the rest of her possessions.

She became a Franciscan tertiary, a religious affiliation in which she kept her status as a laywoman while striving to imitate the religious dedication of Franciscan nuns. Soon Angela began to experience intense mystical raptures. As word spread of her ecstasies and the spiritual insights that accompanied them, other tertiaries—male and female—gathered around Angela to learn how to love and serve God better.

It was still early in Angela's new life when she made another pilgrimage, this time to Assisi. While praying in the Basilica of St. Francis she had a brief vision of Christ. When the Lord vanished Angela shrieked, "Love still unknown! Why? Why? Why?" Collapsing on the church floor, Angela went into convulsions, all the while uttering loud, unintelligible sounds. As it happened her relative Father Arnoldo had been assigned to the basilica; he was among the handful of friars who, hearing the commotion, hurried into the church. When Arnoldo saw a member of his own family writhing on the floor, concern gave way to anger and humiliation. Once Angela was herself again, Father Arnoldo scolded her for giving in to hysteria, making a spectacle of herself and embarrassing him in front of his brother Franciscans. He commanded her never to come back to Assisi.

Angela submitted and stayed away from Assisi, but

Angela's good works among the poor, the sick, and the sinners of Foligno touched the priest's heart. He joined her circle, acting as a chaplain to the group and serving as Angela's scribe until her death in 1309.

The people in and around Foligno always venerated Angela as a saint, yet the case for her canonization was never introduced in Rome. Nonetheless, in recognition of her sanctity and three hundred years of veneration, in 1693 Pope Innocent XII confirmed this devotion to Angela by granting her the title "Blessed."

St. Ignatius of Loyola, Egotist

[1491–1556]   FEAST DAY: *July 31*

Ignatius of Loyola grew up in his father's castle
dreaming of chivalry. Family history told how in 1321
his ancestors, the seven sons of Juan Perez de Loyola,
drove an army of French and Navarrese from their
Basque homeland. But there were more recent exam-
ples of heroism to inspire him. Ignatius's father, Beltran,
had distinguished himself fighting for Ferdinand and
Isabella in their final push to drive the Moors from
Spain. And Ignatius's older brothers (he was the
youngest of thirteen children) covered themselves in
glory fighting in France, Naples, and the Low Countries.

His oldest brother, Juan, even sailed with Columbus on the explorer's second voyage to the New World, where he died in battle against the Indians. Stirred by these deeds of valor in his own family, Ignatius longed to sacrifice himself for a great king, to faithfully serve a beautiful lady, and to win immortal fame in the eyes of the world.

By the time Ignatius was out of his teens, he had adopted all the qualities of a cavalier: he was ambitious, vain about his appearance, prickly regarding his honor. Juan de Polanco, Ignatius's secretary and one of his earliest biographers, tells us that at this time Ignatius was "addicted to gambling and dissolute in his dealings with women." When Ignatius and another courtier, Francisco de Oya, quarreled over who had the right to a certain lady's favors, de Oya swore to settle the matter by killing Ignatius. For the next year Ignatius went everywhere armed, waiting for de Oya to make his move, spoiling for a duel that would end either with his death or his rival's.

Of course, Ignatius could not win glory as a strutting courtier alone; he had to prove himself in battle. When he was twenty-six years old he got his chance. Ignatius had entered the service of Antonio Manrique de Lara, Duke of Najera and viceroy of Navarre, a province that both the Spanish and the French claimed as their own. Ignatius was in Pamplona when the French attacked the city. Faced with an army of twelve thousand Frenchmen and batteries of heavy artillery, the city council did the pragmatic thing and surrendered. But Ignatius did not. He rallied the garrison of the citadel to disregard the surrender and fight the invaders. Pamplona's surrender was meaningless if the city's stronghold remained in Spanish hands. With no other option, the French attacked the citadel. For the next six hours Ignatius was in his element, leading a desperate, hopeless defense against vastly superior numbers and the relentless pounding of French artillery. When a portion of the fortress wall collapsed, Ignatius drew his sword and leapt into the breach, ready to win fame at last. As Ignatius stood on the pile of rubble, waiting for the onslaught, a cannonball passed between his legs, shattering one and wounding the other. When Ignatius fell, the garrison's courage collapsed. They surrendered to the French commander, who played his part in this chivalric pageant by sparing the lives of the defenders and sending his personal physicians to treat Ignatius.

After two weeks the doctors believed Ignatius was strong enough for the journey home. A team of soldiers placed the wounded hero on a litter and escorted him back to his family's castle. He was still basking in the praise of his family when the physicians the Loyolas had summoned delivered some bad news. The leg shattered by the cannonball had been improperly set; it would have to be broken and set again. Bear in mind, at this time Western medicine had no anesthesia. Ignatius was fully conscious when the surgeons went to work on him. Writing about it later, he described the procedure as "butchery."

Still, the legs did not heal as Ignatius expected they would. The shattered leg was now shorter than the other one. Even worse was how the other leg had mended—with an unsightly lump of bone protruding just below the knee. Ignatius refused to limp, and would not tolerate a deformity. He commanded the surgeons to saw off the offending lump of bone and stretch his other leg—again, without anesthesia.

During the long, agonizing weeks that followed Ignatius's sister-in-law Magdalena nursed him. When he was improving but still bedridden, he asked her for some novels to read. Magdalena owned only two books, and both were religious classics of the Middle Ages: a life of Christ written by Ludolph the Carthusian and Jacobus de Voragine's collection of saints' lives, *The Golden Legend*. With nothing else to amuse or distract him, Ignatius started reading.

Ignatius's conversion progressed every time he turned a page. He felt deeply ashamed that he had let vanity, pride, lust, and violence rule his life. Then he had an inspiration. He could still pursue the chivalric ideal by serving the King of Heaven, pledging undying love to Our Lady, and striving to win souls for God. The course of his future life was confirmed for him one night in August or September 1521 when the Blessed Virgin and the Christ Child appeared in his room.

In February 1522, when Ignatius's legs were well and strong again, he made a pilgrimage to the shrine of Our Lady at Montserrat. There he hung his sword and dagger on the grill before the altar of the Blessed Virgin, then kept a nocturnal vigil, in deliberate imitation of the ceremony in which a gentleman prepared for knighthood by spending the night in prayer.

Ignatius had a well-developed sense of gallantry, but in terms of the spiritual life he was immature. He spent the next year with Dominican friars, learning the basics of religious formation. As he read and studied, he began to develop his own ideas on how a man could live for God. Later he would bring these ideas together in a book, the *Spiritual Exercises*, a work that is not only the cornerstone of the training of a Jesuit, but also the basis for the contemporary religious retreat movement. The Ignatian ideal urges the Christian to shake off the desire for comfort and success and become a new person impatient to do God's will no matter how difficult, unpleasant, or even dangerous it may be.

Ignatius wrote his *Spiritual Exercises* as a handbook. It takes thirty days for a retreatant to complete the exercises, and with each new day come fresh challenges to examine his actions, his motivations, and his desires, and to give up any attachment that might hold back spiritual development. While other spiritual classics are inspirational, the *Exercises* is practical: it is a method detailing how to change one's life by altering one's perspective—from doing what makes one happy to doing what is pleasing to God.

Ignatius had no formal education, so he enrolled at the University of Paris to study theology. His roommates were two other theology students, St. Francis Xavier and St. Peter Faber. Under Ignatius's influence both men abandoned their plans for worldly careers in favor of a life dedicated to God. Five more students joined this little circle of friends to form an informal community of men zealous to work for the greater glory of God. On the Feast of the Assumption, August 15, 1534, Ignatius and his seven friends met in the crypt of the chapel of Saint Denis in Paris's Montmartre district. Faber, the only priest among them, said Mass. Then, before they received Holy Communion, they all recited personal, informal vows of poverty and chastity. They weren't thinking of founding a religious order yet, but they did want to do something to bind themselves more closely together. If people asked who they were, they said they were the Compania de Jesus, in Latin the Societas Jesu, in English the Society of Jesus. Or, as they are best known, the Jesuits.

In November 1537 Ignatius, Faber, and their fellow Jesuit James Lainez set out for Rome. Once Ignatius had offered to fight for the Duke of Najera; now he was offer-

ing his services to Pope Paul III. In a chapel outside the
Eternal City Ignatius had a vision in which he heard God
the Father promise, "I will be favorable to you in Rome."
And he was. The Jesuits impressed Paul III. He assigned
Faber and Lainez to teach theology and scripture at
Rome's Sapienza University and encouraged Ignatius to
follow his own ad hoc mission of preaching and teaching.

In Rome Ignatius and his companions refined their
vision of themselves. They saw themselves as teachers
and defenders of Catholic doctrine and as the particular
servants of the pope, ready to go anywhere he felt they
could do good. On September 27, 1540, Pope Paul III
gave formal approval to the Society of Jesus. Not sur-
prisingly, by a unanimous vote the Jesuits elected
Ignatius the first general of their order.

During the last fifteen years of his life Ignatius saw
the Society of Jesus grow from eight to one thousand
members with seventy-six houses in twelve provinces
across the globe—including Brazil, Japan, and India. In
an effort to turn back the effects of the Reformation, he
opened a Jesuit seminary in Germany.

Rome was sweltering under a heat wave in July
1556 when Ignatius fell ill with a stomach complaint.
The doctor assured him it was nothing to worry about.
On July 30 Ignatius felt very ill, but kept his discomfort
to himself. He did, however, ask his secretary, Juan de
Polanco, to take a message to the pope requesting a
papal blessing on Ignatius and the Society of Jesus.

Polanco replied that he had several important letters to write that day; he would go see the pope tomorrow. "I would be pleased more today than tomorrow, or the sooner the better," Ignatius said. "But do what you think best in the matter."

The sun was just coming up the next day when the infirmarian made a perfunctory call on Ignatius and was shocked to discover his superior all alone and in his death throes. Polanco raced to the Vatican, but by the time he returned Ignatius Loyola had died—without the papal blessing, or even the last rites.

St. John of God,
Gambler and Drunkard

[1495–1550]   *FEAST DAY: March 8*

St. John of God's biographers have always been suspicious about an incident that occurred when he was eight years old. A man who claimed to be a wandering priest stopped at the home of John's parents, Andrew and Theresa, in the Portuguese town of Montemor-o-Novo, near the ancient city of Evora. John and his family were poor peasants who owned a few sheep and worked a few acres of land. They were not important; they had no powerful friends. So the next morning when Andrew and Theresa discovered the stranger had vanished, taking their little boy with him, there was no one they could turn to for help.

As there is a longstanding tradition of sanitizing the lives of the saints, readers who look up St. John of God in a standard collection of saints' lives may encounter this excuse: the priest's tales of his exciting life on the road fired the wanderlust of little John. The next morning, when John begged the departing houseguest to take him along on his adventures, the priest, being a softhearted fellow, agreed.

If, by some slim chance, this is how John's disappearance from home actually played out, one can't help asking why the stranger did not at least run the idea by Andrew and Theresa. And then there is the matter of how the story ends. At a town in Spain called Oropresa, some sixty miles west of Toledo, the priest left John with a family of strangers. He made no effort to get John home, nor did John ever see the man again.

The whole story smells fishy. Most likely John was forcibly abducted, possibly even seduced by the stranger.

As for John's distraught parents, a few months after his disappearance his mother died—of a broken heart, the neighbors said. With both wife and child gone, John's father gave up the farm to join a community of Franciscans as a lay brother.

Meanwhile, in Oropresa, John was safe and happy. The Count of Oropresa employed John's foster father as one of the managers of his estates. Since John had a little experience as a shepherd, he was put to work guarding the count's flocks. The new family—we do not know their name—accepted John as one of their own, cared for him, loved him. The man John came to regard as his father was devout; he taught John to say twenty-four Hail Marys every day, one for each year of Our Lady's life after Christ's Ascension.

As John approached manhood he felt restless. The routines of working the count's estate bored him; he longed for excitement. When King Charles V declared war on France, John enlisted in the army. As a twenty-two-year-old raw recruit he was eager to prove to seasoned veterans that he was as much a man, as much a soldier as they were. He adopted all the vices of the camp: swearing, gambling, heavy drinking, and visits to prostitutes. A word about swearing in the sixteenth century: all the foul terms we hear today were in use five hundred years ago, but with a difference that made swearing much worse. In the Middle Ages and the Renaissance it was common to pair up vulgar obscenities with the names of God, the Virgin Mary, and any saint the swearer thought of at the moment.

John's army career ended in disgrace. He had been assigned to watch a cache of plundered valuables but left his post. In his absence a portion of the loot was stolen. Some of the officers wanted John hanged for dereliction of duty, but a senior commander intervened, gave John a dishonorable discharge, and sent him home.

The shame of being thrown out of the army marked the first step in John's long process of conversion.

Back in Oropresa, John still longed for excitement, but he also began to toy with the idea of doing something with his life that would be pleasing to God. At one point he went to Ceuta, a city in Morocco recently captured by Spain, with the idea of ransoming Christian slaves from the Moors. There he met a poverty-stricken Portuguese family whom he decided to support. He found a job building the city's fortifications. Convicts brought over from Spain made up most of the workforce, and the foremen at the building site did not ask who was a free man and who was a criminal: they beat anyone they thought was slacking off. For the convicts there was only way to escape such a brutal, degrading sentence—run away to the Moors and convert to Islam. John had gotten to know one convict who gave up his Catholic faith to win his freedom. The man's apostasy preyed on John's mind until he almost believed that he, in some inexplicable way, had contributed to the convict's decision to deny Christ. He disclosed his qualms of conscience to an elderly Franciscan chaplain, who recognized an excessively scrupulous penitent when he heard one. He assured John the runaway convict was responsible for his own decisions, that for John to blame himself was a perverse form of pride. Concluding that it was spiritually dangerous for a man as sensitive as John to continue working where so many men succumbed to despair, the priest commanded him, for his own good, to go back to Spain at once.

In Spain John drifted from odd job to odd job. At last he settled on selling religious books and holy pictures out of a small shop he opened in Granada. The business enjoyed modest success; his neighbors respected him as an honest, sincerely religious man. But John remained obsessed with his own sinfulness.

In January 1537 St. John of Avila, a renowned mystic and fiery preacher, came to Granada to preach on the feast of St. Sebastian, January 20. The guest preacher's reputation attracted a large congregation, and John was among the crowd that day. In the middle of the sermon a high-pitched wail echoed through the church. Howling like a wounded animal, calling on God to forgive his sins, John stumbled through the congregation and out the church door. He ran through the city streets beating his breast, tearing his hair, half mad with the thought that he was damned. After several days of this, the town authorities had John locked in an asylum. There John of Avila visited him. Calmly but firmly he told John to give up hysterics. If he wanted to please God, he must find something useful to do.

Once John was released from the asylum he did not have to look very far to find good work that needed doing. Like every other city in Europe, Granada had hospitals, orphanages, and shelters for the poor—but not enough. John rented a house and turned it into a hospital for the poor with forty-six beds. Initially no one came forward to help him. No doubt his hysterical outburst on St. Sebastian's Day made any would-be volunteers think twice. He did all the work himself: he nursed his patients, did the laundry, cooked the meals, cleaned the wards, even hiked into the hills to collect firewood. To get the food and supplies his hospital needed, John begged in the streets. Carrying a large basket he walked through Granada crying, "Who wants to do good to himself? Do good to yourselves, brothers, for the love of God!"

It took time for the inhabitants of the city to overcome their assumption that John was out of his mind. Slowly, benefactors rallied around, donating the essentials John needed to run his hospital. In time doctors and nurses offered their services, free of charge.

Now John expanded his work, opening a shelter for the homeless, caring for the elderly, finding foster mothers for orphans, and work for the unemployed. The hospital remained his primary work, however, and he had a regular team of assistants who worked in the wards. Church authorities in Granada recognized their efforts by giving the men a religious habit. As for the founder, in recognition of his sanctity, the churchmen urged him to take the name John of God.

Toward the end of his life John wrote a brief letter to a young man outlining what was necessary to be an effective nurse in his hospital. "You will have to work more than you have been used to," John said, "but you will have the consolation of doing all for God. Be zealous in the service of the poor and be ready to sacrifice even your skin. Have God continually before your eyes and love him above all things."

St. Camillus de Lellis, Cardsharp and Con Man

[1550–1614]   FEAST DAY: *July 14*

Camilla and Giovanni de Lellis had many children, but only one child, a boy they named Camillus, survived infancy. He should have been the joy of the family, but young Camillus gave his mother nothing but trouble. He got into fights with the other boys in the neighborhood. He skipped school. He learned his prayers, but wouldn't say them. As a little boy Camillus defied his mother; when he was older he intimidated her. By the time he was twelve years old, Camillus was so tall, so strong, and so quick to unleash his violent temper that Camilla was actually afraid of her own son.

The distraught woman received no help from her husband. In the first place, Giovanni was rarely home. He was a mercenary soldier by profession, and the wars that flared up across Europe in the sixteenth century kept him fully employed. Some mercenaries at this time fought for a cause; Giovanni de Lellis fought for the money. In 1527 Emperor Charles V was offering the highest price to mercenaries who fought for him in his war against Pope Clement VII. Although an Italian and a Catholic, Giovanni signed on with the emperor and participated in that orgy of murder, rape, and sacrilege known as the Sack of Rome.

Camillus was twelve or thirteen when his mother died. Giovanni couldn't care for him, so he passed into the custody of relatives. They had no more success taming Camillus's unruly disposition than his mother had. At age seventeen Camillus left his relatives' house to join his father as a mercenary for the Venetians in their war against the Turks. Standing over six feet tall and powerfully built, Camillus was a recruiting officer's dream.

The typical vices of a military camp—swearing, drinking, whoring—Camillus picked up quickly. From his father, however, the young man learned how to gamble and the art of the con. Moving from camp to camp, from war to war, and working as a team, father and son supplemented their pay as mercenaries by fleecing their fellow soldiers.

The de Lellis men were between wars when, unexpectedly, Giovanni fell seriously ill. Once the realization came to him that he would not recover, that he was dying, Giovanni sent his son to fetch a priest. After the old mercenary made a good confession, repenting of all his sins and crimes, he received Holy Communion for the last time and died.

Camillus was stunned. He had heard of deathbed conversions. In the camps and on the battlefields he may have even seen one or two. But the idea that his own father would repent, call for a priest, and die in a state of grace probably never occurred to Camillus as even a remote possibility.

Nonetheless, his father's conversion made an impression on Camillus. He decided he would convert, too. One of his uncles was a Franciscan in Aquila; Camillus resolved to go there, give up his life of sin, and spend the rest of his days as a pious, humble brother of St. Francis.

If Camillus's uncle thought his hulking nephew's sudden desire to enter the religious life was funny, he kept it to himself. The other friars in the house were kind to Camillus and let him stay for a while, but suggested that he wasn't mature enough in his judgment to commit himself to a religious order.

The friars were right. No sooner had Camillus left them than he started gambling again. About this time he suffered a minor injury just above one ankle, which ulcerated and would not heal. Since the wound meant Camillus could not go back to soldiering, he supported himself as a gambler.

He kept on the move, and his ulcerated leg kept getting worse. In Rome he dragged himself to the Hospital of San Giacomo, where he made the brothers who ran the place an offer: if they tended his leg and gave him a bed and meals, he would work as a servant in the wards. Such an arrangement was commonplace in sixteenth-century hospitals. Moved by a combination of charity and practicality, the religious orders who operated the hospitals routinely took in vagrants to do the dirty jobs and heavy lifting so the brothers or nuns could devote themselves to tending their patients.

The dishwashers and floor scrubbers were as tough as Camillus: in such company it was easy to get a card game going. But once those dishwashers and floor scrubbers noticed that Camillus was winning a few too many hands, they accused him of cheating. The resentment among Camillus's victims bubbled over into bickering and then brawling, until at last the hospital administrators threw Camillus out.

With no other options, he became a mercenary again. Over the next two years Camillus fought in Croatia, Naples, Sicily, and North Africa. When the wars were over he tried his hand again as a professional gambler, but luck deserted him. He lost all his money, then his sword, his pistol, even his coat. When he wandered into the town of Manfredonia he was a penniless drifter who owned nothing but the clothes on his back. And he was only twenty-four years old.

Camillus was begging at a church door in Manfredonia when a wealthy gentleman, famous locally for his good works, spotted the tall, well-built young man and made him an offer. He was the patron of a new monastery that was being built outside town. The builders needed a man to do odd jobs—would Camillus be interested? With no other options presenting themselves, Camillus accepted the offer.

At the construction site Camillus did all the most tedious jobs: he loaded building stones on donkeys, ran errands, brought meals to the craftsmen. He hated the work, but he stayed, and in time he began to acquire two virtues he had never tried to cultivate before: self-discipline and responsibility. When the monastery was finished Camillus set out again for Rome, heading straight for San Giacomo's hospital. Touched by Camillus's promises of good behavior, the brothers gave him a second chance.

It was while he was working at San Giacomo that Camillus had an opportunity to introduce himself to St. Philip Neri. The most famous priest in Rome, Neri was spearheading a reawakening of religious life in the city. After listening to the onetime mercenary and compulsive gambler's story, Neri agreed to serve as Camillus's personal spiritual director.

The routine of work at the hospital coupled with the spiritual direction from Philip Neri steadied Camillus. Unlike his halfhearted efforts in the past, Camillus felt that this time his conversion was sincere and permanent, and he began to look around for some way to be useful to God and man that was a bit more ambitious than cleaning the San Giacomo kitchen. Hospital work seemed the natural choice. The poor neighborhoods of Rome were crammed with sick folk who had no one to care for them and no place to go for help. And his experiences at San Giacomo gave him definite ideas of what a hospital should and should not be. He rented a house near the Tiber River in a miserable part of the city and fitted it out as a hospital for the poor.

Camillus was euphoric about his new project, but Neri was skeptical. He reminded Camillus that he had barely succeeded in banishing his evil companions and sinful habits, that the neighborhood he had chosen was filled with exactly the types of temptations to which he had always been most susceptible. The smartest thing Camillus could do was cancel the lease on the house, go back to work at San Giacomo, and wait until his religious formation was stronger.

Camillus rejected Neri's advice. In return Neri said that if Camillus would not listen to sound spiritual counsel, he could no longer act as Camillus's spiritual director. He even went so far as to refuse to hear Camillus's confessions in future. It broke their friendship, and marked one of the rare occasions when St. Philip Neri's assessment of a man's character was dead wrong. Camillus did not slip back into his old sins; his hospital proved to be a great success. Both priests and laymen volunteered to work with him. As for the hospital itself, Camillus introduced a program of innovations that set the standard for health care in Rome. The wards were well ventilated, the patients were served healthy meals, and those suffering from contagious diseases were quarantined. And Camillus went a step further. Unlike the other hospitals of his day, which sought to give the desperately ill a clean, comfortable place to die, Camillus and his staff tried to cure their patients.

The last thirty years of his life Camillus spent nursing the sick and opening new hospitals, yet as he lay dying, he was anxious that his old sins might outweigh his good works. Shortly before Camillus died the superior of the Carmelite friars visited him. "Pray for me," Camillus begged the man, "for I have been a great sinner, a gambler, and a man of bad life."

In his final hour, Camillus's confidence in God's mercy was restored. He stretched his arms out so his body took the form of a cross, and giving thanks for the Blood of Christ that had washed away his sins, he died.

St. Camillus de Lellis lies buried in the little Church of Santa Maria Maddalena in Rome. In 1886 Pope Leo XIII named him patron saint of nurses.

St. Philip Howard, Cynic and
Negligent Husband

[1557–1595]   FEAST DAY: October 19

Of all the religious upheavals that shook Europe in
the sixteenth century, Henry VIII's was the most cunning. Although he cast off the authority of the pope and
made himself Supreme Head of the Church in England,
Henry insisted that he was still a Catholic. He retained
the Mass, as well as all seven sacraments, and even insisted that priests remain celibate. Henry's most violent
attack on traditional religion—aside from his judicial
murder of St. Thomas More, St. John Fisher, and the
Carthusian Martyrs, among others—was the dissolu-
tion of the monasteries and the destruction of England's

shrines. Yet Henry's reasons for this sacrilege were political. By dismantling the abbeys and the shrines he satisfied the radical Protestant faction in his government,
and he enriched his treasury with the treasures of the
Church. As for the monastic lands, he used them as
bribes, parceling them out to the noblemen of England,
buying the loyalty even of those noble families who
wanted to remain faithful Catholics.

Today the Howard family, whose head is the duke of
Norfolk, ranks first among England's Catholic peers.
But when Henry VIII, and then Edward VI, and then
Mary I, and finally Elizabeth I were on the throne,
the Howards were not so forthright about their faith.
Throughout the Tudor period, they adjusted their consciences to fit the religious mood of the moment. In fair-
ness to the duke of Norfolk, there was a lot riding on
keeping in the king's good graces. The Howards were
the most powerful, and among the wealthiest, members
of the English aristocracy. In terms of bloodline, their
claim to the English throne was actually a little better
than that of the Tudors, who were, after all, descended
from an upstart Welsh archer. Thomas Howard, the
third duke of Norfolk, had followed every twist and
turn of Henry's religious, marital, and political policy.
True, at the end of Henry's reign the duke had been imprisoned in the Tower of London on a charge of treason,
but even then his luck held steady—Henry died, and the
duke was released.

The fourth duke followed his father's playbook. He was a staunch Protestant under Edward VI, a repentant and devout Catholic under Mary I, then a loyal Anglican when Elizabeth I wore the crown. It must come as no surprise that his son and heir, Philip Howard, grew up cynical and hedonistic.

Initially Philip was brought up as a Catholic. Queen Mary attended his baptism, where her husband, Philip II of Spain, was named the infant's godfather. The duke engaged Dr. Gregory Martin, a learned and pious Oxford scholar, to tutor his son, but when Elizabeth I's Parliament gave her Henry VIII's title, Supreme Head of the Church in England, then passed the Act of Uniformity requiring all English subjects to attend church services that followed the Book of Common Prayer, the duke changed his religion as easily as he changed his shoes. The Catholic Dr. Martin left the house, to be replaced by Anglican chaplains and tutors.

Dr. Martin did not remain unemployed long. In 1570 he crossed the English Channel to enroll in the English Catholic seminary at Douai and subsequently was ordained a priest. A brilliant linguist, he was invited to join a select panel of five scholars to translate St. Jerome's Latin Vulgate version of the Bible into English.

At age twelve Philip was married to Anne Dacre, daughter of Lord Thomas Dacre. Two years later the young couple was married again, at the insistence of Philip's father. At the time the duke was locked away in the Tower of London on suspicion of treason. He feared the queen, in a vindictive mood, might annul Philip and Anne's marriage. If they went through the ceremony a second time, however, it demonstrated that they had given their full consent twice, which, the duke hoped, would place the marriage bond safely beyond the breaking point.

At age fifteen Philip went to the university at Cambridge, where a wealthy student from the most influential family in the land could expect to become a target for sycophants. These thoroughly unpleasant young men introduced Philip to the taverns, the brothels, and the gambling houses of the town. They flattered him extravagantly, and he believed it all. Years later the memory of those sycophants still made Anne blush with shame.

After three years at the university Philip left for Queen Elizabeth's court. Once again Philip found himself surrounded by people eager to win his favor. They offered him bribes—money, gold, jewels—and, vain and weak-willed courtier that he was, he took them. The court was full of sexually adventurous young women, and it appears that Philip accepted what they offered, too. About this time he stopped going home to visit Anne, and even stopped writing to her. Soon he was saying openly that he did not know if he was truly married.

His maternal grandfather, the earl of Arundel, and his aunt, Lady Lumley, tried to draw him away from his evil habits, but he treated both with such contempt that they revised their wills and left property that would have gone to Philip to other members of the family.

To win the favor of the queen Philip staged elaborate tournaments to celebrate the anniversary of her coronation. On another occasion he invited the queen and the court to his home, entertaining them in the most lavish manner for several days. In spite of his inherited wealth and the bribes he had been taking, such extravagance drove Philip deep into debt. To rebuild his fortune, he had to sell part of his estate and part of Anne's property, too.

In 1581 Philip Howard attended a debate in the Tower of London that pitted a panel of Protestant theologians against a single Jesuit priest, St. Edmund Campion. Brought up a Protestant, Campion had studied at Oxford, where he performed so brilliantly that Sir William Cecil, part of Elizabeth I's inner circle, proclaimed the young man "one of the diamonds of England." After he entered the ministry, however, Campion began to have doubts about the Anglican Church. He slipped out of the country, taking a roundabout route to Douai, where he was received into the Catholic Church and then began studying for the priesthood.

After his ordination Father Campion joined the Jesuits, who sent him back to England to serve as a clandestine missionary. He brought the Mass and the sacraments to the persecuted Catholics of the country and worked to persuade Protestants to return to the Catholic faith. After a little over a year in England, Father Campion was arrested, imprisoned in the Tower of London, and tortured repeatedly on the rack. Now he was compelled to participate in a public religious debate. He requested books that he might prepare for the contest. They were denied. The Protestant theologians, however, had brought to the debate a small library of texts for their own reference. In spite of these disadvantages, Campion defended the Catholic position eloquently, scoring more points against his opponents than they scored against him. When it became obvious that the sympathies of the spectators were shifting to Campion, the government cancelled the debate. By that time, however, Father Campion had unknowingly awakened the conscience of Philip Howard.

Soon a rumor was circulating in the court that the young earl was about to become a Catholic and planned to join the English Catholic exiles on the Continent. Before Philip could act he received word that the queen was coming to visit him at his residence in London, Arundel House. He planned a sumptuous banquet that delighted Elizabeth. The next day, instead of sending her thanks, she sent Philip a message that he must remain at Arundel under house arrest. Philip was so closely watched that three years passed before he could safely arrange a meeting with a Jesuit father, William

Weston, so both he and Anne could make their confessions and be received back into the Catholic Church.

By this time the life of Catholics in England was near impossible. Successive acts of Parliament had made it treason to call the queen a heretic, to even discuss who might succeed her at her death, or to bring papal documents into the country. It was treason for an English Catholic priest ordained overseas to return home, and it was treason to help or house a Catholic priest. And the penalty for treason was horrible: the traitor was hanged by the neck but cut down while still alive and conscious. Next his genitals were hacked off, his chest cut open, and his heart ripped out. Finally, he was beheaded and his body chopped into four quarters, which were displayed wherever the monarch pleased. In 1535, after the Carthusian prior St. John Houghton suffered this grisly death, Henry VIII had one of the martyr's arms, with the shoulder attached, nailed over the entrance to his monastery, a bloody lesson to the monks and passersby of what happened to dissenters who refused to recognize the title Henry had usurped for himself.

Of course, there were lesser penalties for lesser crimes. To hear Mass or to receive the Catholic sacraments was a crime punishable with imprisonment. Catholic parents faced prison if they had their child baptized a Catholic, or tried to send their children to Catholic schools on the Continent. Priests who said Mass in England were hauled off to prison, where they were tortured to reveal the places where they had stayed and the names of the people who had attended their Masses.

Then there were the financial penalties. Anyone who missed Protestant services was fined twenty pounds a month—an amount that would bankrupt a working family in two or three months. To bring into the country "crosses, pictures, beads or such like vain and superstitious things," as the act of Parliament put it, would cost the importer his land and all his goods. The same punishment applied to whoever received these holy objects.

Parliament's reach extended even to within the privacy of the family: one statute made a Protestant husband liable if his Catholic wife refused to attend services at the Anglican parish church.

Unwilling to compromise their faith, and fearful of what might become of them if they tarried in England, Philip and Anne resolved to flee the country. Since Anne was pregnant, Philip would go first and she would follow later. He hired a ship to spirit him quietly out of England, but government agents had been watching the young earl. His ship had barely left port when it was stopped and boarded, and Philip was arrested. He was taken to the Tower of London and fined ten thousand pounds for the offense of trying to leave England without the queen's permission. For the next five years he remained a prisoner in the Tower, left in a legal limbo with no charges preferred against him, until the Spanish Armada's failed invasion gave Elizabeth's government the excuse it had been waiting for to charge Philip with treason. After a farce of a trial he was found guilty and sentenced to death. The sentence was never carried out. Elizabeth appeared satisfied to let Philip rot in the Tower.

For the last six years of his life Philip designed a monastically inspired routine, dividing each day into periods of study, exercise, and prayer. He fasted three times a week. Since he was forbidden a crucifix, he scratched one into the wall. When the Jesuit priest St. Robert Southwell was arrested and confined in the Tower, the two prisoners sent letters back and forth between their cells.

In August 1595 Philip fell ill with a serious case of dysentery. When it became obvious he was dying, he sent a message to the queen, begging her permission to see a priest. She refused. She also refused to let him see Anne, his son, or his brothers. When Philip died, only his servants and his jailers were at his bedside.

Not long before he sent a letter to Anne. "I call God to witness," he wrote, "it is no small grief unto me that I cannot make recompense in this world for the wrongs I have done you; for if it had pleased God to have granted me longer life, I doubt not but that you should have found me as good a husband . . . by his grace, as you have found me bad before . . . [God] knows that which is past is a nail in my conscience."

St. Peter Claver, Dithering Novice

[1580–1654]   FEAST DAY: *September 9*

Slavery was ubiquitous when Jesus Christ was on earth. To the people who lived two thousand years ago, the notion that an economy could operate without slaves was unthinkable, just as we cannot imagine an economy without employees.

Although Christ never said a word about slavery, his saying from the Sermon on the Mount, "All things therefore whatsoever you would that men should do to you, do you also to them" (Matthew 7:12), certainly could be applied to it and would in time be the primary religious argument for slavery's abolition.

When the apostles went out from Jerusalem to preach the gospel, they made no distinction been slaves and the freeborn. Men and women, whatever their condition, were welcomed into the Church. St. Paul put it best when he wrote, "There is neither Jew nor Greek; there is neither bond nor free; there is neither male nor female. For you are all one in Christ Jesus" (Galatians 3:28). Whether they were conscious of it or not, by recognizing that in the eyes of God all human beings were equally worthy of salvation, the apostles were undermining the foundations of slavery.

In Europe, at least, slavery died out over time. By the twelfth century it was virtually unknown. Then, in the fifteenth century, the European exploration of Africa, Asia, and the Americas revived the moribund slave trade. The Portuguese explorers who followed the coast of Africa in search of new trade routes to Asia saw moneymaking opportunities everywhere they went. With their superior weapons, it was easy to conquer local people, and it was a short step from subduing a population to enslaving them. As one of the first "new lands" colonized by the Portuguese, the Canary Islands became the first place where slavery was reintroduced. When word of the situation reached Pope Eugenius IV in 1435, he fired off a letter to Bishop Ferdinand on the island of Lanzarote, denouncing the enslavement of the Canary Islanders and demanding that they be set free. He gave the Europeans on the islands fifteen days to liberate their slaves or incur the penalty of excommunication.

As the Portuguese and then the Spanish pushed farther and farther into fabulously wealthy unknown lands, the temptation to exploit the riches of these territories through the slave labor of the local population became irresistible. But, as people will do, the slavers came with a rationale for their actions: it was justifiable to enslave the American Indians, Africans, and Asians because they were less than human. Pope Paul III demolished that argument in 1537 when he published a document, *Pastorale Officium*, which asserted that "the Indians themselves indeed are true men" and that "no one in any way may presume to reduce said Indians to slavery." In spite of papal condemnations, the international slave trade flourished among Catholics and Protestants for another four hundred years.

About this time a son was born to the Clavers, a farming family who worked the land in the province of Catalonia in northeastern Spain. The parents named the boy Peter. He was bright and deeply religious but found it hard to make a decision and stick with it. His parents sent Peter to a school run by the Jesuits in Barcelona. The Jesuits were still a relatively new religious order in the Catholic Church; their founder, St. Ignatius of Loyola, had organized them in 1534. Yet even at this early stage they had a reputation as skillful teachers and trainers of young minds. The Jesuits were also renowned as missionaries: in Europe, by their preaching, their debates, and their publications, the Jesuits were pushing back the Reformation and bringing Protestants and fallen-away Catholics back to the Catholic Church; in foreign lands—the Americas, India, and Japan—they were bringing a rich harvest of new converts into the Church. The Jesuits were so famous for their intellectual achievements that people tended to overlook their works of charity. Yet Jesuits worked in hospitals and prisons and even served as chaplains to the slaves on the galley ships.

Such an active, exciting life appealed to Peter. He had many conversations with the Jesuits at his school about entering the Society of Jesus, but in spite of all the encouragement he received from the good fathers Peter was reluctant to commit himself. After vacillating for several years, Peter Claver asked to be received as a Jesuit novice.

At the Jesuit college of Montesión at Palma on the island of Majorca, Peter began his studies in philosophy. He had barely entered the novitiate when he began to second-guess himself. What if he was not cut out for an active life as a missionary or parish priest? Maybe his true calling was as a monk. Peter's endless doubts and misgivings must have been maddening for his fellow novices, to say nothing of his confessor and his religious superior. Fortunately, help was nearby.

The porter at Montesión was a seventy-two-year-old

lay brother named Alphonsus Rodriguez. Brother Alphonsus had had a family and a career, but after his wife and children all died, he gave up his business and entered the religious life. Although he was a Jesuit brother now, he hadn't lost his ability, cultivated over many years as a businessman, to judge character. Nor had he lost his knack for handling a customer who couldn't decide what he wanted.

Peter confided his doubts to Brother Alphonsus, who assured him he belonged with the Jesuits. Moreover, Brother Alphonsus thought Peter should ask his superiors to send him to the Americas as a missionary. Peter was stunned. But Brother Alphonsus insisted the way to overcome fear and indecision is make a bold move.

So Peter summoned up his courage and asked his superiors to assign him to the American mission. They gave their consent but suggested he should be ordained a priest first.

That was more commitment than Peter could bear. All his doubts about his religious vocation surfaced again, and once again he waffled. Perhaps the Jesuits at Montesión saw more in Peter than he saw in himself; perhaps Brother Alphonsus convinced them the life of a missionary was precisely what Peter needed; perhaps they just wanted him to go become someone else's headache. Whatever their reasons, in 1610 they let Peter have his way and sent him to Cartagena, Colombia, unordained.

Cartagena's location on the Caribbean Sea made it one of the principal ports for the slave trade in the New World: twelve thousand enslaved Africans were unloaded in Cartagena every year. After weeks crammed together in the dark holds of the slave ships, these tragic people were filthy, weak from hunger and dehydration, and half mad with fear. Many were sick. Some were dying. Yet, whatever their condition, all were driven into holding pens near the dock to be sorted out and sold later.

The only white man who treated the Africans kindly was a Jesuit priest, Father Alphonsus de Sandoval. When he heard the roar of the harbor cannon that signaled the arrival of another slave ship, Father de Sandoval gathered up food, water, and medicine and hurried down to the harbor. The comforts Father de Sandoval could offer the Africans were meager, yet he cared for his "parishioners" day after day until they had all been sold off and the pen was empty.

When Peter Claver, the apprehensive new Jesuit recruit from Spain, arrived in Cartagena Father de Sandoval made him his assistant. At first glance it would appear that the priest had made a terrible mistake. Yet the work in the slave pen transformed Peter. Once he recognized that he could do something for God and his fellow man, all doubts, all qualms, all uncertainties vanished. He asked his superiors in Cartagena to ordain him and to permit him to serve the slaves.

Peter's zeal surpassed even Father de Sandoval's. Every time a slaver sailed into Cartagena's harbor, Peter took the pilot's boat out to the ship and began his work at once down in the hold. On shore, as sailors and soldiers herded the slaves into the pens, Peter went with them. Over the years he built up a team of interpreters who could speak the languages of Guinea, the Congo, and Angola, the lands from which most of the captives came. Through his interpreters Peter tried to comfort the Africans and learn what they needed. Every day Peter and his interpreters returned with more food, more water, more medicines, and as he treated the Africans, he explained to them the basics of the Catholic faith. It is said that during the forty-four years Father Claver served in the slave pens, he baptized three hundred thousand Africans. It is impossible to assess if that number is accurate.

Whatever the number of converts may have been, Peter regarded them as his parishioners. True, he could not do anything for those who were sold to distant plantations, settlements, and mines. But he could serve those Africans who were put to work in Cartagena or at locations just outside the city. Father Claver kept up a steady round of visitations, saying Mass for his converts, bringing them the sacraments, and continuing their religious instruction. While he was there he reminded the masters of the law that forbade slave owners to split up slave families.

Father Claver's devotion to his African converts enraged the white population of Cartagena. Church authorities heard complaints that Father Claver was keeping slaves from their work, contaminating churches and chapels with his congregations of unwashed Africans, profaning the Blessed Sacrament by giving Communion to "animals." Some well-born ladies refused to enter a church if Father Claver had said Mass there for slaves. Even some of Peter's brother Jesuits thought he was excessively devoted to the Africans. Yet after years of wavering Peter Claver had found his vocation, and he would not be deterred from it.

Peter kept up his exhausting routine until one day, when he was seventy-four years old, he collapsed in the slave pen. Back at the Jesuit residence Peter lay on his deathbed, abandoned by the white Christians of Cartagena. The only one who tried to nurse the dying man was an African servant. The end came quickly. Late in the evening on September 7, 1654, Peter Claver received the last sacraments, then fell unconscious and died shortly after midnight. A crowd of slaves broke down the gates of the Jesuit residence so they could see their saint one last time.

On January 15, 1888, the people of Rome witnessed a double canonization as Pope Leo XIII declared that Peter Claver and Alphonsus Rodriguez were saints.

Venerable Matt Talbot,
Chronic Alcoholic

[1856–1925]   *ANNIVERSARY OF HIS DEATH: June 7*

By 1856, the year Matthew Talbot was born, the population of Dublin stood at a quarter million, of whom sixty-four thousand fell into the general category of poor folk. Dublin in the mid-nineteenth century had some of the modern conveniences that were beginning to appear in Europe and the United States: city water systems; indoor toilets known as water closets, or at least outdoor privies for each house; and new housing designed to bring natural light and fresh air into every room.

In the poor parts of dear, dirty Dublin, however, these innovations were unknown. Water for cooking, drinking, and washing came from public fountains, which did not run twenty-four hours a day. Few places had privies, fewer still had water closets, so human waste was carried in buckets to be dumped somewhere outdoors. The houses themselves tended to be tenements crammed into narrow alleys and dank, sunless, airless courtyards.

The Talbot family never knew the grinding poverty of some of their neighbors: as a dockworker Charles Talbot brought home fifteen shillings a week, supplemented from time to time by a few extra shillings Elizabeth Talbot earned as a cleaning woman. She rarely had time to work outside the house, however. In twenty-five years of marriage Elizabeth Talbot gave birth to twelve children, nine of whom survived into adulthood. Matthew was the Talbots' second child.

With the exception of the eldest son, John, all the Talbot men were heavy drinkers. In old age Pat Doyle, who had grown up with the Talbot children, recalled that once the Talbot boys were young men they went to pubs together with their father. "On Saturdays," Doyle said, "when they'd all have a good drop in . . . they were a contrary lot. Mrs. Talbot had a hard time of it, trying to keep the peace."

In fact, Matt did not wait for manhood to begin drinking. He was twelve the first time he stumbled home drunk. His father beat him, then got him a job at the docks where he could keep an eye on his son. But even at this young age Matt always found ways to get to a pub. When the Archdiocese of Dublin began the process of investigation into Matt's life, two of his sisters, Maria and Susan, testified that he would sell his boots and shirt to get money for liquor. Pat Doyle remembered going on pilfering expeditions through the neighborhood with Matt to find small things they could sell to buy drink. In testimony before the canonization tribunal, Annie Johnson, Matt's niece, said that when his money was gone her uncle would get drunk on credit. When he could get no more credit, he would steal. Once he stole an old homeless man's fiddle and pawned it to buy liquor.

From the time he was twelve until he was twenty-eight, Matt Talbot was a chronic alcoholic. One Saturday evening he and his two youngest brothers, Philip and Joseph, walked to O'Meara's pub on Dublin's North Strand. They had no money, so they stood outside the door, waiting for friends to offer to buy them a drink. One acquaintance after another passed Matt by, but not one asked him in. To his brother Joe he said, "I am going home."

His mother was surprised to see him come through the door early and sober. "I am going up to Holy Cross College," he told her, "to take the pledge." At that time in Ireland, anyone who resolved to give up drink took a solemn oath, or pledge, before a priest. Elizabeth Talbot was delighted but realistic. "If you don't intend to keep it, don't take it."

At the college Matt told the officiating priest that he wanted to take the pledge for life. The priest, who had experience with alcoholics, suggested that Matt swear off drink for three months. If he could make it that far, then he could return to take a second pledge for a longer period, and so on.

While he was with the priest, Matt made his confession, his first in several years. The next morning he went to Sunday Mass, received Holy Communion, and began a new routine that he said kept him out of the pubs. Every morning he attended 5:00 A.M. Mass, then went to his job—he was a laborer at construction sites—arriving about 6:00 A.M. After quitting time he would walk to a church at some far corner of Dublin and remain there until it was time to go home for supper and bed.

Matt's friends were astonished when he swore off the booze. As for Matt, he had a bad time during those first three months—so bad that he told his mother when the three months were up, he was going to start drinking again.

But he didn't. At the end of those three months he returned to Holy Cross College to take another short-term pledge. How long these incremental pledges lasted we do not know. A woman named Catherine Carrick left a written statement that she served Matt Talbot "his last pint of porter before taking the life pledge." Sadly, she didn't include a date. But she did add that once, after Matt had sworn off alcohol, he stopped by the pub to see her. "He told me," Carrick said, "he would never touch drink for his life."

It was a marvel to all who knew him that Matt Talbot had given up the bottle. It was a wonder to him, too, one that he attributed entirely to the mercy of God and the intercession of the Blessed Virgin. He began to consider how he could atone for his wasted, sinful years, and how he could grow closer to God. Matt took as his models the Irish saints from the early centuries of Christianity. They had spent long hours in prayer, passed most of the year fasting, slept on stone slabs with a rock for a pillow. Matt Talbot adopted all of these penitential practices. He prayed so often that his sister Maria said it seemed to her "he was never off his knees." He slept on a wooden plank with a block of wood as his pillow. During Lent he lived on dry bread, a little fish, and unsweetened cocoa. To prepare for Christmas he gave up meat during Advent. His sister Susan said when Christmas morning came, Matt savored the steak she fried for his breakfast—the first piece of meat he had tasted in four weeks.

He adopted one other act of humiliation he considered particularly necessary: he paid off all the debts he owed to friends and coworkers who had bought him drinks, and he paid back the pub owners who had let him drink on credit. Several people bore witness that he scoured all the poorhouses of Dublin, trying to find the old man whose fiddle he stole so he could make restitution. He never found him.

Matt had a small circle of friends, and he was close to his family, particularly his sisters. He and his brothers drifted apart after he failed to convince them to give up, or least moderate, their heavy drinking. He lived with his mother until she died, then he rented a room, which he furnished in austere style with a bed, a table, and a chair. Since he had so few needs, he gave the bulk of his salary to charities, or to acquaintances and neighbors who were going through hard times. And every morning he was at the earliest Mass, usually arriving at the church before the doors had been unlocked.

In 1923 Matt suffered severe chest pains and was taken to Dublin's Mater Misericordiae Hospital. He was diagnosed with tachycardia, an abnormally rapid heartbeat. No longer able to do the heavy lifting at construction sites, Matt received seven shillings a week from Ireland's National Health Insurance. Even for someone who lived as simply as Matt, the disability payout was barely enough. Friends stopped by to press him to accept small gifts of cash, and the St. Vincent de Paul Society, one of Matt's favorite charities, was now writing him checks.

June 7, 1925, was Trinity Sunday. Matt was hurrying to Mass at St. Savior's Church on Dominick Street when he collapsed. Several passersby rushed to his aid, while a Mr. O'Donohoe, who owned a pub, ran for a priest. Matt died there on the sidewalk, surrounded by kind strangers.

The funeral was small. Matt's sisters Maria and Susan and their families attended, and a few friends from work came, as did a handful of his fellow members of the Sodality of the Immaculate Conception. In life, Matt Talbot's sanctity was known only to a select few. Since his death, his reputation for holiness has traveled around the world, but he is especially loved and admired by recovering alcoholics.

Bibliography

Anderson, Alan Orr, and Marjorie Ogilvie Anderson, eds. and trans. *Adomnan's Life of Columba* (Thomas Nelson and Sons, 1961).

"The Arabic Gospel of the Infancy of the Saviour," *The Ante-Nicene Fathers*, Vol. 8, http://www.ccel.org/-fathers2/ANF-08/anf08-75.htm#P6477_1928435.

Armstrong, Regis J., and Ignatius C. Brady, *Francis and Clare: The Complete Works* (Paulist Press, 1982).

Armstrong, Regis J., J. A. Wayne Hellman, and William J. Short, *Francis of Assisi: Early Documents* (New City Press, 1999).

Augustine, *Confessions,* translated by Henry Chadwick (Oxford University Press, 1992).

Barlow, Frank, *Thomas Becket* (University of California Press, 1986).

Bitel, Lisa M., *Isle of the Saints: Monastic Settlement and Christian Community in Early Ireland* (Cornell University Press, 1990).

The Book of Saints, 6th ed. (Morehouse Publishing, 1989).

Bowden, Henry Sebastian, *Mementoes of the Martyrs and Confessors of England and Wales*, edited and revised by Donald Attwater (Burns & Oates, 1962).

Brown, Peter, *Augustine of Hippo: A Biography* (University of California Press, 1969).

Bury, J. B., *The Life of St. Patrick and His Place in History* (Book-of-the-Month Club, 1999).

The Catholic Encyclopedia (1913; electronic version, New Advent, 1997), http://www.newadvent.org/cathen.

Clarke, W. K. Lowther, *The Lausiac History of Palladius* (Macmillan, 1918).

Cross, Samuel H., ed., *Russian Primary Chronicle: Laurentian Text* (Medieval Academy of America, 1968).

Davies, Oliver, with Thomas O'Loughlin, trans., *Celtic Spirituality* (Paulist Press, 1999).

Delehaye, Hippolyte, *The Legends of the Saints: An Introduction to Hagiography* (University of Notre Dame Press, 1961).

Demetrius of Rostov, *The Great Collection of Lives of the Saints,* Vol. 2, *October* (Chrysostom Press, no date).

de Voragine, Jacobus, *The Golden Legend*, 2 vols. (Princeton University Press, 1993).

Dorcy, Sister Mary Jean, *St. Dominic's Family: The Lives of Over 300 Famous Dominicans* (Tan Books, 1983).

Duffy, Eamon, *Saints & Sinners: A History of the Popes* (Yale University Press, 1997).

Duffy, Eamon, *The Stripping of the Altars: Traditional Religion in England 1400–1580* (Yale University Press, 1992).

Farmer, David Hugh, ed., *Butler's Lives of the Saints*, 12 vols. (The Liturgical Press, 1995–2000).

Bibliography

"Fathers of the Church," in *The Catholic Encyclopedia* (New Advent, 1997), http://www.newadvent.org/fathers.

Fitzgerald, Allan D., ed., *Augustine Through the Ages: An Encyclopedia* (William B. Eerdmans, 1999).

Fraser, Antonia, *Faith and Treason: The Story of the Gunpowder Plot* (Nan A. Talese, 1996).

Freeze, Gregory L., *Russia: A History* (Oxford University Press, 1997).

Goodier, Alban, *Saints for Sinners* (Image Books, 1959).

Griffin, T. L., *The Life of Philip Howard, Earl of Arundel, Saint and Martyr*, adapted from *The Lives of Philip Howard, Earl of Arundel and Ann Dacres, his Wife*, by the Duke of Norfolk (1857 manuscript), electronic version, 1998, http://www.geocities.com/griffin81au/Howard-Martyr.html.

Grimal, Pierre, *The Concise Dictionary of Classical Mythology*, edited by Stephen Kershaw from the translation by A. R. Maxwell-Hyslop (Basil Blackwell, 1990).

Harrington, Daniel J., *The Gospel of Matthew* (The Liturgical Press, 1991).

Haskins, Susan, *Mary Magdalen: Myth and Metaphor* (HarperCollins, 1993).

Howatson, M. C., ed., *The Oxford Companion to Classical Literature*, 2nd ed. (Oxford University Press, 1989).

James, M. R., trans., "The Gospel of Nicodemus, or Acts of Pilate," in *The Apocryphal New Testament* (Clarendon Press, 1924).

Jerome, "Letters" (no. 77), in *The Catholic Encyclopedia* (New Advent, 1997), http://www.newadvent.org/-fathers/3001.htm.

Jesch, Judith, *Women in the Viking Age* (The Boydell Press, 1991).

John Chrysostom, "Sermon 67 on Matthew," *Nicene and Post-Nicene Fathers,* Series 1, Vol. 10, http://www.ccel.org/-fathers2/NPNF1-10.

Jones, Gwyn, *A History of the Vikings* (Oxford University Press, 1984).

Kelly, J.N.D., *Jerome: His Life, Writings and Controversies* (Harper & Row, 1975).

Kieckhefer, Richard, *Unquiet Souls: Fourteenth Century Saints and Their Religious Milieu* (University of Chicago Press, 1984).

LaChance, Paul, trans., *Angela of Foligno: Complete Works* (Paulist Press, 1993).

Leys, M.D.R., *Catholics in England 1559–1829: A Social History* (Sheed and Ward, 1961).

"The Life of Our Holy Mother Mary of Egypt," Internet Medieval Sourcebook, Paul Halsall, ed., http://www.fordham.edu/halsall/sbook.html.

MacDonald, Iain, ed., *Saint Patrick* (Floris Books, 1992).

Martindale, C. C., *Life of St. Camillus* (Sheed and Ward, 1946).

Maxwell, John Francis, *Slavery and the Catholic Church* (Barry Rose Publishers, 1975).

McMahon, Norbert, *The Story of the Hospitallers of St. John of God* (The Newman Press, 1959).

Meany, Mary Walsh, "Angela of Foligno: A Eucharistic Model of Lay Sanctity," in *Lay Sanctity, Medieval and Modern: A Search for Models*, edited by Ann W. Astell (University of Notre Dame Press, 2000).

Meissner, W. W., *Ignatius of Loyola: The Psychology of a Saint* (Yale University Press, 1992).

Bibliography

Ogg, Frederic Austin, ed., *A Source Book of Mediaeval History: Documents Illustrative of European Life and Institutions from the German Invasions to the Renaissance* (1907; reprinted by Cooper Square Publishers, 1972).

Panzer, Joel S., *The Popes and Slavery* (Alba House, 1996).

Poulos, George, *Orthodox Saints*, 4 vols. (Holy Cross Orthodox Press, 1990).

Purcell, Mary, *Matt Talbot and His Times* (The Newman Press, 1955).

Roy, James Charles, *Islands of Storm* (Dufour Editions, 1991).

Sturluson, Snorri, *Heimskringla: History of the Kings of Norway*, translated by Lee M. Hollander (University of Texas Press, 1964).

Urry, William, *Thomas Becket: His Last Days*, edited with an introduction by Peter A. Rowe (Sutton Publishing, 1999).

Weinstein, Donald, and Rudolph M. Bell, *Saints & Society: The Two Worlds of Western Christendom, 1000–1700* (University of Chicago Press, 1982).

Wiedemann, Thomas, *Emperors and Gladiators* (Routledge, 1995).

Woods, David, trans., "The Passion of St. Christopher." *Bibliotheca Hagiographica Latina Antiquae et Mediae Aetatis*, no. 1764, 1999.